Breakthrough

Unleashing the Power of a Proven Plan

Breakthrough

Unleashing the Power of a Proven Plan

Randon A. Samelson

978-0-578-14838-0

TABLE OF CONTENTS

DEDICATION

The late Fred Smith Sr. was a faithful friend, wise mentor, and courageous critic. Because of these and other virtues, he helped many—most of whom he never met! Fred, we miss you.

ENDORSEMENTS

"*Breakthrough* is simply that—a *breakthrough* for leaders! Brilliant and biblical, this six-step planning model is concise, yet comprehensive. The wisdom and insights are PowerPoint-worthy, but delivered with humility and life-in-the-trenches experience. I'm enthusiastically recommending *Breakthrough*."

-John Pearson
President, John Pearson Associates, Inc.

"Without reservation, I commend the reading and rereading of *Breakthrough*. This book is more than a volume of information; it's a manual for action."

-John Edmund Haggai
Founder, Haggai Institute

"The older I get the more I love two things—the Bible and elegant simplicity. *Breakthrough* combines these two in a way that yields a profound guide for living and leading well, in just about any arena of life. Short and powerful, this book will be worth reading every year to remind me of certain foundational, biblical truths."

-Scott Bolinder
Executive Vice President, Biblica

"*Breakthrough* is a resource that is clear, concise, and well-written. I loved its insights on how David's words and actions can help us in leading our ministries today. Thank you, Randy, for your direct approach and focus on the basics of transparency, honesty, character, and wisdom."

-Doug Lockhart
SVP Bible Marketing and Outreach, HarperCollins Christian Publishing

ACKNOWLEDGEMENTS

❋ Thanks to Lyn Cryderman, whose mind and writing skills helped craft the message of *Breakthrough,* and who in the process became a friend, trusted for his integrity and wisdom.

❋ Thanks to Len Crowley and Dave Forbes, whose initial reaction to the subject and its source spurred the desire to write *Breakthrough.*

❋ Thanks to Jeannie Cox and Dee Martz, without whose help *Breakthrough* would have never been completed.

❋ Thanks to Scott Bolinder, Jack Modesett Jr., Chelsea Samelson, Linda Samelson, Fred Smith Jr., and Mark Taylor, who made *Breakthrough* better.

❋ Thanks to Mark Taylor, Dr. Scott Harrison, and Joni Eareckson Tada for setting a good example and allowing us to share a story about them in the Appendix.

CHAPTER ONE

TURNING DREAMS INTO REALITY

"Behold, I had a dream . . ."
JUDGES 7:13

"Go confidently in the direction of your dreams."
HENRY DAVID THOREAU

EVERYONE HAS DREAMS. Dreams empower and motivate. They can transform people, churches, companies, communities, nations, and even the course of history.

Imagine what our world would be like if the Wright brothers hadn't dreamed about flying. If Thomas Edison hadn't dreamed about a source of light to replace candles and gas lanterns. If Jonas Salk hadn't dreamed about a vaccine to prevent polio. What if Martin Luther King Jr. hadn't dreamed about a nation that lived out its stated belief that *all men are created equal* or if Billy Graham hadn't dreamed about preaching the gospel to the entire world?

I believe we all, at one time or another, desire to accomplish something great—something beyond ourselves. It is this inner desire that drives men and women to climb dangerous peaks, discover cures for diseases, and compose majestic symphonies. Not every dream changes the world, but it can change your world. Yours may be to graduate from college, run a small business, or start a ministry to provide clean water to African villages. Whatever your dream, no matter how big or small, the template in this book will help you. And I have come to realize that when your dream aligns with the gifts and talents God has given you, pursuing that dream will give you great joy.

Dreams are powerful and personal. They grab you, and you're unsure whether you hold them or they hold you. But only a dream that is profoundly personal will evoke the passion and energy essential to surmount the many struggles required to turn it into a reality. Martin Luther King Jr. believed so passionately in his dream that he was willing to die for it, and eventually he did.

But most dreams get stuck somewhere along the way to becoming reality. "Stuck" is where dreams go to die.

This book is about the process of turning dreams into

reality and what to do when you get stuck. In these pages, I offer the rediscovery of a 3,000-year-old template to help you break through the barriers that will inevitably confront you.

MY DREAMS

I've had many dreams over my lifetime. When I was nine years old, I happened to pick up a copy of the newspaper and as I read through it, my eyes stopped on a page filled with numbers. Every other page had sentences, but this one contained mostly numbers and strange combinations of letters that made no sense to me. I asked people about this puzzling page. I eventually learned this was the daily report of how businesses were valued. It was the stock market report.

For whatever reason, those numbers sparked something inside me that led to a dream to earn money while doing something that was fun, like solving a puzzle. I was hooked. So I studied the stock market diligently; at age twelve, I started my own stock account using the money I had earned delivering newspapers. I bought five shares of Cessna and five shares of Lockheed. From that point on, I was fixated on investing. I went on to study business with an emphasis on finance and investing at the University of Michigan. In my twenties and thirties, I joined several futures exchanges in Chicago and New York. My dream of making investing my livelihood came true; to this day, it is my passion.

But dreams don't always come true. Sometimes our dreams are beyond our control—like one of my own. As a young man, I also wanted to someday play basketball in the NBA. In college, after securing a basketball scholarship, I suffered a serious shoulder injury that abruptly and painfully ended my dream to become a professional basketball player.

I have another dream now, one I did not have as a youth. This one has developed over time. My goal is to help Christian ministries and donors reach their own dreams though a non-profit company, Counsel & Capital, which I founded in 1999. My vision is to create a nonprofit "investment bank" serving Christians pursuing biblical priorities, free of charge. Its mission is invigorating Christian ministries and donors by advocating biblically-based principles of governance and giving.

There are ministries all over the world working to feed starving babies, cure the sick and dying, comfort the hurting and lonely, and bring people everywhere the news of Christ. There are donors who share these same desires. I want to help them both meet such needs.

Along the way, my dream for Counsel & Capital has gotten

stuck a few times. I have used the very same template I offer here to keep moving toward its final reality.

A BIBLICAL MODEL: DAVID AND THE TEMPLE OF GOD

Over the years, I have learned to rely on the Bible. Its teachings and themes are incredibly consistent, even though sixty different people wrote it in three different languages across three continents over a period of fifteen hundred years. Even non-believing historians agree that the cities and events recorded in the Bible are accurately described. According to the renowned archeologist Nelson Glueck, not a single archeological discovery has contradicted the truths of the Bible.

Yet curiously, in our modern world, many people view the Bible as irrelevant. Even Christians who say they believe every word often look for guidance elsewhere for the practical challenges of their lives. Men and women today are turning to self-help books for advice and to the latest fads and trends for solutions to their problems. Often, these new and improved, instant-relief solutions do not work.

It may be thousands of years old, but the Bible is tried and true and has withstood the test of time. I find one Bible story in particular especially useful when it comes to pursuing dreams. It's the story of David and his dream to build a temple for God.

Most people, even non-Christians, are familiar with the story of David and Goliath. But few people have studied the compelling details of David's life that make him such an important biblical character, as well as the basis of this book.

David was an ordinary man. He was small and humble and came from a family of sheep farmers. After he killed the giant Goliath, he won the favor of the Israelite king, a man named Saul. David eventually married this king's daughter, became his advisor, and ultimately became King himself. The Bible says that David was "a man after His [God's] own heart" (1 Samuel 13:14), but David was far from perfect. He committed adultery with Bathsheba, and then arranged for the murder of her husband. One of David's sons died, another son raped his half-sister, and another son rebelled against David and seized the throne.

David's life was incredibly messy, chaotic, and full of failures, just as we sometimes view our own lives. In spite of David's human frailty and imperfections, God used him to accomplish great things. Even near the end of his life David dreamt of building a great temple, a place "where the Ark of the Lord's covenant, God's footstool, could rest permanently" (1 Chronicles 28:2).

The Ark of God (also, Ark of the Covenant) is the most sacred relic of ancient Israel. It was an elaborate, gold-covered chest containing mementos of the forty years of the nation's wilderness wanderings. During those years in the desert, God proved Himself a faithful provider and protector of His people. The Ark was a physical link to the presence of "the Lord Your God" (Exodus 20:2), as He is known in the Old Testament. It was placed in a restricted room called the Holy of Holies, which symbolized the place where God met the people personally and therefore reminded them of His authority, righteousness, justice, and compassion.

At that time, the Ark was carried from place to place. Without a home, it resided inside a large, tent-like structure called the Tabernacle. After more than four hundred years on the move, David wanted to build a permanent dwelling for the Ark of God, the Temple. This was his dream.

Building this structure was a huge and highly ambitious project that would take time, work, energy, skill, and leadership. It was no simple task. There were no bulldozers or cranes or Home Depots. And yet, over many years, the workers completed the Temple. David's dream came true.

The process David and his successor and son Solomon followed, as recorded in the Bible in 1 Chronicles 28-29 (see chapter nine, "Straight from Scripture"), is the same six-step template that you can apply to your dream. It has worked for me, and I invite you to discover how it can work for you.

Do you have a dream, something you really want to accomplish that never seems to make it beyond your wish list? What are you willing to do to make it come true? Are you achieving it? Have you even begun to reach for it? Are you stuck? If so, explore with me the ancient wisdom that can turn your dream into reality. Let's start by recognizing there may be an obstacle in your path. I call it the *key log*.

Chapter Two

FINDING THE KEY LOG

". . . first get rid of the log . . ."
MATTHEW 7:5 (NLT)

"If I had an hour to solve a problem I'd spend fifty-five minutes thinking about the problem and five minutes thinking about solutions."
ALBERT EINSTEIN

I N THE PACIFIC Northwest, logging has been a major industry for over a hundred years. *Real* axe men wrestle heavy chainsaws to fell giant pine trees that are then pushed and pulled by snarling bulldozers until the massive logs pile high along the top of a riverbank. With a final shove, the whole pile goes cascading down the bank and into a fast-moving river that acts as a superhighway. The logs float miles downstream to an offloading dock where towering cranes pluck them from the water and gently stack them onto flatbed railroad cars or trucks.

It's an effective system that has been in place since the beginning of the logging industry in the United States, dating back to the early nineteenth century. When it works, it's the picture of efficiency, saving the loggers from having to transport the unwieldy trees down treacherous paths carved into the steep terrain.

Every now and then, however, the stream of logs in the river gradually slows down before coming to a complete stop, threatening the goal of delivering this particular batch to the lumberyard. Somewhere along the journey downstream, something got in the way and the logs began piling up, creating a logjam.

Savvy loggers jump into action, literally dancing over the treacherous logjam, each one looking for the same thing: the key log. With years of experience, loggers discovered if they could find that one log causing the problem and remove it, the logs would float downstream again. Today, using satellite imagery and computer analysis, loggers are able to identify the key log much faster than their counterparts of earlier days. But the concept is the same. Find the key log, remove it, and everything becomes unstuck.

When my friend Fred Smith Sr. first told me about the key log concept, I immediately thought of the many individuals and organizations I've worked with. They have a noble goal or mission. A dream. They want to accomplish something not just for the sake of accomplishment but for the sake of the Kingdom. So they make the decision to go for it: metaphorically, they put the logs in the river and float them downstream. And eventually — it always happens — somewhere en route to their goal they get stuck — and discouraged. They wonder if they should lower their expectations or set smaller goals. Some even consider quitting. Many eventually do.

Through years of experience working with people who get stuck, I've learned the best way to get them unstuck is to help them find the key log, that one barrier that, if removed, would allow them to continue toward the success they desire. Locating that key log and developing a plan to remove it will release their full potential. So I developed a key log question that I ask every person or leader of an organization that is stuck: "What one opportunity or obstacle, if captured or removed, would most advance your vision?"

Invariably, their answer is money. "If we just had more money, we could accomplish our goal." Or, "We could do so much more for God if we could find an infusion of capital." And you know what? Money is rarely the key log. It's almost never the barrier. In just about every instance where I sit down with a ministry leader to discuss the situation, lack of money is not the problem. Instead, the major reason is tied directly to a failure to follow the template revealed by King David in 1 Chronicles 28–29 when he and Solomon built the Temple of God.

The Temple, the land, and its location in Jerusalem have arguably been the focal point of world history for much of the last thirty-five hundred years. It was an extraordinary physical accomplishment at the time. Its symbolism and inspirational impact cannot be overestimated.

The location of Solomon's Temple has become the most contested religious site in the world. At least four religions ultimately have used what is now called the Temple Mount: Judaism, Christianity, the Roman Religion, and Islam. It remains the bullseye of the Arab/Israeli conflict. Most would argue that the site and the creation of the original Temple are important to everyone.

Given that fact, it seems wholly logical that one would pay particular attention to any messages that might be gleaned from the process used to build it. I believe the Bible suggests there was a six-step solution. It drove David and Solomon from a vision to the ultimate destination. Those six steps were:

1. Inspiring Vision

2. A Credible Plan

3. The Right Leader

4. Initial Funding

5. Going Public

6. Sharing Credit

You may read the entire account starting on page 141 with commentary.

The key log that blocks so many organizations from reaching their full potential is usually a shortcoming in one of those six areas. Although money is involved in two of the six steps, as mentioned before, the key log is rarely money.

For example, a few years ago the CEO of a well-respected Christian ministry sought my counsel because his organization had plateaued and he wanted to find a way to increase his donor base. At the time, the ministry's annual budget hovered around $5 million. He felt they were stuck. He wanted the ministry to grow, and he had an idea of how to do it.

"I'd like to buy a series of radio spots sharing powerful stories about how the Bible has changed people's lives," he explained. "We've collected stories from all over the world, and by airing them, I believe we'll elevate our profile and increase awareness about the importance of reading the Bible. But my board won't approve the project."

I liked his idea. Radio is a powerful medium, and personal stories always inspire people. So I asked him to show me his plan. He didn't have one. He had a compelling vision. I considered him to be an effective leader. But that's never enough to accomplish great things. His key log was the lack of a clear and coherent plan to guide the organization into radio.

Once King David committed to his vision of building the Temple, he couldn't just snap his fingers and watch it get built. Nor could this very capable CEO effectively use radio to grow his ministry by just announcing to his staff that they were going on air. So I told him I would help him and his leadership team develop a plan to promote their radio ministry. First, he'd need to address some questions. Who would oversee the process? Would they produce the stories in-house or hire a professional studio? Whom were they trying to reach? What markets would deliver their target audience?

What would the cost-benefit analysis be? I believed so much in the power of a credible plan to break through the key log, I went a step further.

"If you develop a comprehensive plan for this initiative, I will advance you half the budget as seed money," I explained. "If you don't reach your goal, you can keep the money. If you reach or exceed your goal, you can pay me back with no interest so these funds can be used to help someone else." He seemed a bit surprised at my offer but thanked me, and over the next few weeks, we put together a plan to present at his ministry's next board meeting. This time, the board gave him the green light, as well as the remainder of the money he needed to move forward with a radio promotion. Now here's the good news: the series of radio spots netted twenty-two thousand new donors and communicated wonderful stories with impact. It was not long until the ministry's annual budget grew from five million dollars to forty million!

When you discover the key log — the one thing blocking your progress — you will have a much greater chance of breaking through and getting unstuck. Money wasn't the issue for this CEO. Even if initially he had been able to get the board to give him the funds he asked for, he might still be stuck, and that money would have been squandered despite his good intentions. Without a plan, it is possible this ministry would be very different today with a much smaller impact.

I've seen this happen again and again — with organizations, with individuals, with entrepreneurs, even with my own children. They always think if they could just get their hands on more money, they would accomplish their goals. But when they do a little fact-finding based on these six important steps David used in 1 Chronicles 28–29, they usually find the key log.

So how do you find your key log? Following are three options to consider:

1. **Study chapters three through eight of this book and the underlying Bible text in chapter nine.**

   The more you understand about the importance of the process David and Solomon used to build the Temple in Jerusalem, the more likely you'll be able to find your own key log.

   If you or your organization seems to have plateaued, and you can't get past your current situation, review the six steps of David's approach to build the Temple. Do you have a clear vision for what you want to do, for where you want to go? Have you developed a plan — a roadmap — to show you how to get to your destination? Do you have the right leader in place and the right people in the right jobs? Do you have the proper funding to implement this plan? Have you effectively communicated your vision to those who can help you accomplish it? And are you willing to share the credit among those who helped get the job done?

2. Seek wise and appropriate counsel.

CEOs and individuals pursuing dreams can reap extraordinary benefit in having outside support. For the CEO ministry leader, it's important to keep his or her board informed and have great relationships. But often those relationships are not detached enough to hunt effectively for a key log.

Develop a relationship with an experienced and wise person who is somewhat detached from your individual or organization's dream. The ministry leader might not be able to "see the forest for the trees." Distractions and day-to-day responsibilities get in the way. Therefore, a second or third party is essential. Once you find one or two appropriate counselors, keep them updated regularly. Don't wait until a crisis breaks out.

3. Monitor Counsel & Capital's website.

I encourage you to visit *counselandcapital.org* for relevant articles or insights. Also, if the first two solutions don't get the job done, please contact us so we might help you personally with your organization's needs.

It may seem overly simple or obvious to go through these steps. And it might seem a bit old-fashioned to go to the Bible for the answers to the problem you're facing. But the Bible is the greatest source of wisdom to which we can turn. It was given to us for our good if we would only apply it.

You can buy every book on management or leadership. You can — and should — get as much training and education as you can. But in my opinion, it will all be in vain if you don't make the Bible your priority as a reliable guide for your life and your work. It is wisdom that is literally God-breathed just for you.

Now let's look at the six steps. As you do, be alert for your own key log, the place where your dream could die or where you could begin to unleash the power of a proven plan.

BREAKTHROUGH

CREATING AN INSPIRING VISION

*"It was my desire to build a temple where
the ark of the Lord's Covenant,
God's footstool, could rest permanently."*

1 Chronicles 28:2 (NLT)

*"If you don't know where you're going, you
might wind up someplace else."*

Yogi Berra

A s a young cartoonist, Walt Disney was a failure. The newspaper he worked for fired him because the editor didn't like any of his ideas. Following that, no one would buy his cartoons, so he took a job at a small church drawing illustrations for their advertising. The pay was so miniscule that he couldn't afford an apartment, so the church let him sleep in a mouse-infested garage next door. He gave one of the mice in that garage the nickname Mickey, and the rest, as they say, is history.

By the time Disney World in Orlando, Florida, opened in 1974, Walt had passed away. Veteran broadcaster Walter Cronkite covered the opening on television with Mrs. Disney sitting next to him. At one point during the broadcast, he leaned over to Mrs. Disney. "Wouldn't it be great if Walt were here to see this today?"

"If Walt had not first seen this," she replied, "you would not be seeing it today."

Walt Disney could have remained stuck in the throes of rejection and failure, but he saw something no one else could see—an empire built around a lowly rodent. Your effectiveness as a leader starts with a clear and inspiring vision. Or as Carl Sandburg once said, "Nothing happens unless we first dream."

IDENTIFYING A VISION

What exactly is a vision? When I think of a vision or a dream (to me, the terms are interchangeable), I think of a desire that is so captivating that it lifts us beyond our human limitations. A proper vision captures the heart. It breeds passion and promotes perseverance during difficulties.

As John P. Kotter wrote in *Leading Change*, "Vision refers to a picture of the future with some implicit or explicit commentary on why people should strive to create that future." A clearly stated vision or dream allows everyone to know where an individual or organization is headed. To be most useful, such a vision needs to be written clearly and succinctly. Kotter believes a good vision statement serves three important purposes: one, it clarifies the general direction; two, it motivates people to take steps in the right direction; and three, it helps to quickly and effectively coordinate the actions of numerous people.

There is something irresistibly appealing about an inspiring vision. Back in David's time, no one had ever attempted to build a temple. Some would say it was an impossible task. But when David shared his vision for the Temple, it inspired the leaders of Israel to give "freely and wholeheartedly to the Lord" (1 Chronicles 29:9).

In my thirty-five years of advising individuals and organizations on how to turn their dreams into reality, I have observed that few suffer from a lack of vision. But one of the challenges for leaders is to be able to communicate that vision so that it inspires others to embrace it as their own. You probably know what your vision is, but what about others? Have you articulated it? If it's a personal vision, does your spouse or closest friend know it? If you lead an organization, does everyone from the top down understand it?

Physician and social commentator Richard Swenson says:

> A vision is not an arbitrary string of verbiage constructed to fill a vacant morning at the corporate board retreat. It is the foundation for our thoughts, actions, and values. Therefore it is not enough to have a [statement of] vision—we must also live it. Reach higher than tomorrow, higher than the basement, higher than your moods, and higher than your appetites . . . even when it is lonely and even when culture isn't helping. It will be the right decision.[1]

If you have the ember of a worthy dream beginning to glow within you, congratulations! Cherish it. Let it inspire your imagination. Do not let it go. And a wise way to start is to *put it in writing.*

Why write it? The act of writing out your vision or dream tends to give it more importance, which in turn makes you more likely to accomplish it. Psychology professor Gail Matthews of the Dominican University in California conducted a study that showed people who write down their goals are thirty-three percent more successful in accomplishing them than those who do not write them down.[2] In my experience, I've found that the process of putting a dream in writing and carrying it with you as a constant reminder can help provide daily focus, energy, and clarity. Furthermore, a written statement can also be shared with others, attracting them to the power of your dream and enabling you to benefit from their wisdom.

John Bryson, author of *Strategic Planning for Public and Nonprofit Organizations,* believes that a clearly stated vision answers the question, "What will success look like?" He adds that, "It is the pursuit of this image of success that really motivates people to work together."

Great companies understand the value of a clearly stated vision statement. Can you identify the company behind each of these statements?

- To bring inspiration and innovation to every athlete in the world.
- To develop a perfect search engine.
- Our vision is to be the earth's most consumer-concentric company; to build a place where people can come to find and discover anything they want to buy online.
- To give people the power to share and make the world more open and connected.
- To provide fast and easy video access and the ability to share videos frequently.

If you guessed Nike, Google, Amazon, Facebook, and YouTube in that order, you're pretty good! Or maybe *they're* pretty good at writing vision statements that clearly identify what they do.

SIX ELEMENTS OF A WRITTEN VISION STATEMENT

You can find instruction on writing a vision statement from many sources, but none as trustworthy as the Bible. Turning again to David, we learn that the most useful vision statements are personal, inspiring, clear, succinct, measurable, and meaningful.

Personal

Can you imagine trying to cast a vision that you did not own? Unfortunately, it happens. Many visions have been thwarted when difficulties arose because people realized too late that the dream wasn't really their own. Perhaps the idea came from a pastor, parent, or friend. Young people often pursue dreams they think will please their parents. Sometimes newly hired ministry leaders feel as if they must carry out their predecessors' visions even if it requires abandoning their own. That doesn't mean you cannot own a vision that came from another person. David's vision was not Solomon's, but

Solomon would never have been able to build the Temple had he not owned David's. A vision must be personal and it must be yours. If you are pursuing a dream imposed on you or that you don't fully embrace, it's only a matter of time before motivation and enthusiasm disappear.

David made it very clear that the vision to build a temple was *his:* "It was my desire to build a temple" (1 Chronicles 22:7). And when he knew he would not be able to follow through with the project, he prayed that God would give Solomon everything he needed to build the magnificent structure.

Let's assume you lead an organization and you just spent a day in retreat with your board clarifying your vision statement. By the end of the day you had rewritten it. Since this was a joint effort, how can you be certain this new vision is *yours*—that you are not just going along with your board to keep them happy? Trust me, if you do not personally accept this vision and own it with the same commitment and passion as if it were your own, you'll have a difficult time turning it into reality.

If you wonder if your vision is truly yours, find a quiet place where you will not be distracted and sit still until your mind is calm. Then ask yourself, "How would I react if right now I had just been told I could not pursue this dream?" If your first reaction is to protest or express deep disappointment, that's a good indication you've taken ownership of the vision. But if you found yourself breathing a sigh of relief, consider that a warning. Don't sign on for something you do not completely accept as your own.

I also recommend you seek the counsel of one or two very close friends who know you well and have demonstrated they are willing to tell you the truth. Share the vision that has been offered to you and then ask your trusted advisors, "Does this sound like something I could embrace as my own or something I would do only out of obligation?"

By spending time in quiet discernment and then seeking wise counsel, you'll know if the vision placed before you is truly yours.

Inspiring

I remember once talking to a chairman of a board of a bank at a nonprofit event. We discussed the organization sponsoring the event, and the man told me rather abruptly that if the organization's vision didn't inspire him, it wouldn't get his attention or support.

Jack Welch, the former CEO of General Electric, once said, "The best leaders are those who articulate a vision that inspires others." As the writer Antoine de Saint-Exupery stated, "A rock pile ceases to be a rock pile the moment a single man contemplates it, bearing within him the image of a cathedral." The best leaders inspire others to see the cathedral.

King David's vision statement was inspiring because it met a great need. It provided the nation unity, a sense of stability and permanence, and reminded the people of the importance of focusing on God. Extraordinary service to God and man—the need can be great or small—is more likely to evoke passion and thus keep us engaged because we are serving a purpose higher than mere selfish interest. As King of Israel, David was an old man, nearing his death, yet he still was able to inspire the entire nation to undertake this monumental task. After sharing this audacious vision, he asked who was willing to do whatever it would take to build the Temple. According to Scripture, the affirmative response was unanimous and enthusiastic.

Not only was it clear that David was passionate about building the Temple, but his vision statement ignited the passion of others. This is one of the most critical aspects of a vision statement. While no one else may match the visionary's personal passion and commitment, an inspiring vision statement can generate contagious, motivating enthusiasm. This is precisely what happened with David and the nation of Israel. The people not only embraced his vision, but according to the Bible they gave generously to make the Temple a reality: "They gave toward the work on the Temple of God" significant gifts of gold, silver, bronze, and precious stones (1 Chronicles 29:7–8).

Clearly, David's inspiration found its origin deep within his own heart and imagination. He *knew* what he wanted to do. However, if he could not have shared what was inside him with those who would need to be recruited to accomplish the vision, God's Ark might have remained in the mobile, tent-like tabernacle it had occupied for more than four hundred years. The next challenge was to make his vision clear to his people.

Clear

When it comes to your eyes, would you settle for cloudy or blurry vision? Of course not. If your optometrist prescribed a new pair of glasses, and when you put them on you couldn't see clearly, you would likely ask for a refund. When it comes to your dream or vision for you or your organization, you must make it totally clear to everyone.

Suppose someone says to you, "I have a heart for people in Africa who are hurting. I am going to start an organization to help meet the needs." You might respond, "That's great. What region or country would you concentrate on?" The person replies, "Oh, maybe Zambia or Ghana. Perhaps Mozambique." Then you ask what kind of organization the individual has in mind. "One that would develop schools in rural areas, or offer micro-loans to poor entrepreneurs, or maybe teach women a trade."

This person has a vision that is clearly personal and maybe even inspiring to him. It's wonderful that he wants to help hurting people in Africa. But he may have to do it alone because his vision statement lacks clarity. It's too general and vague to motivate anyone to join him. Your vision statement must be as *specific* as possible. Know exactly what you want to achieve. Having a fuzzy vision is a good way to lose sight of the road before you ever get started on your journey.

As Theodore Hesburgh, former president of the University of Notre Dame, once said, "The very essence of leadership is that you have a vision. It's got to be a vision you articulate clearly and forcefully on every occasion. You can't blow an uncertain trumpet."

Succinct

The great management expert, Peter Drucker, reportedly advised that a vision statement should fit on the front of a T-shirt. Excellent advice. The phrase "less is more" has become popular in our society, and for good reason. Excess words, ideas, and images increase the risk of misunderstanding. The key is to follow the advice of Thomas Jefferson: "The most valuable of all talents is that of never using two words when one will do." Make your vision statement short and to the point. David expressed his vision in sixteen words. That was pretty succinct and a good model for the rest of us.

When John F. Kennedy announced to the nation his vision of sending Americans to the moon, he could have rambled on for many minutes about how the space program would advance research and development for all sorts of useful technologies. He could have enumerated how space exploration would give the United States strategic advantage over the Soviet Union, and how a government spending program of that magnitude would invigorate the economy. It is true that his speech did include reasons to expand the space program. But the words we remember, the words that motivated a nation to reach higher than any other in the history of the world, were simple and straightforward: "This nation should commit itself to achieving the goal, before the decade is out, of landing a man on the moon and returning him safely to the earth." Because he kept it succinct, we knew precisely what his vision was for our large and complex space program:

"to put a man on the moon by 1969" (nine words). But what made this statement particularly effective was that it pointed to a meaningful outcome which could be measured.

Measurable

Many dreams are inspirational or aspirational but not measurable. They sound great on paper, but you never know what success would actually look like. Not David's. Everyone knew when his dream was finally realized. The Temple would be completed exactly as David described it. His dream was measurable.

Let's say that you love chess. If you had a choice between being a really good chess player or earning the U.S. Chess Federation title of Grand Master, which would be more valuable to you?

A measurable vision creates enthusiasm for you and for others as you make progress towards achieving the dream. If you are competitive, and you feel the dream slipping away, then a tight, clear, inspiring vision can provide the necessary motivation to keep going.

Finally, it implies accountability. If your dream is vague, it is hard for those who want to support you to assess whether you are on track or not, whether you deserve continued ongoing support or not, and whether there is anything specific they can do to help encourage you.

Meaningful

One of the challenges of developing an inspiring vision statement is to identify a result that you believe others will value. It's difficult to lead men and women on a journey that produces an outcome that has little meaning for them. For example, your vision might be to increase your organization's revenue by twenty percent, but other than your treasurer or finance person, not too many people are energized by increased revenues. What may have greater meaning for them is how you plan to use those increased revenues. Will you feed more children, provide more training, or plant more churches?

King David's vision was important certainly to himself, but also to those he led—the citizens of Israel. The outcomes, if achieved, would be meaningful to them. It would not only give them a grand and magnificent edifice where they could worship God, but also the satisfaction and joy that comes from accomplishing a great thing. At the dedication of the Temple of Jerusalem, the Bible tells us that *all* the Israelites knelt and gave thanks to God, saying, "He is good; his love endures forever" (2 Chronicles 5:13).

Of course, not every vision is a sweeping crusade to tackle

national or global issues. It does not have to be. Even a small-scale dream can make a big difference. Visiting a group of shut-in seniors in your community each week, for instance, could change their world—and yours—in profound ways.

Author and leadership expert John C. Maxwell once wrote, "The great men and women of history were not great because of what they earned or owned. They were great because they gave themselves to people and causes that lived beyond them. Their dream was to do something that benefited others."[3]

What about you? Do you have a vision for your life or for the organization you lead? Is it yours or is it something imposed on you? Does it have the capacity to inspire others? Does it inspire *you?* This is so important, because leadership is lonely and tough. If you're not inspired, how can you inspire others? I recommend that leaders keep their vision statement on an index card and put it on their mirrors so they see it first thing in the morning and carry it with them to inspire them. If you can't stay inspired, you will gradually lose your passion and energy for what you have been called to do.

Don't water down your dream. Fill it with fervor. A well-crafted vision statement can be contagious, a characteristic that is vital to getting your dream off the drawing board and into the real world. There was great, contagious power in

King David's vision statement because it contained all six elements. It was personal, inspiring, clear, succinct, measurable, and meaningful. Do the same with your written vision statement, and you are well on your way to turning your dream into a reality. Then you will be ready to work on a credible plan.

SUMMARY

CHAPTER 3 – CREATING AN INSPIRING VISION

WHY IN WRITING
Increases the probability of achieving the desired result

SIX ELEMENTS OF A WRITTEN VISION STATEMENT

Personal
Engages your personal passion

Inspiring
Helps others to see the cathedral in the rock pile

Clear
Makes it easy to understand

Succinct
Try to use 16 words or less

Measurable
Know when the dream is realized

Meaningful
Makes a difference

BREAKTHROUGH

CHAPTER FOUR

DEVELOPING A CREDIBLE PLAN

"But the noble man makes noble plans,
and by noble deeds he stands."
Isaiah 32:8

"Men don't plan to fail, but fail to plan."
William Segal

I'VE SAID IT before, but it bears repeating because it is so important: organizations fail not because they don't have a vision, but because they have not clearly articulated that vision, or if they have, they lack a plan for turning that vision into reality. This is the place where most visions die. Ninety percent of the ministries and most individuals I work with want to go straight from vision to funding. Yet it is frequently the plan, not money, that will get the desired results. A vision without a plan is merely a delusion. Consider all the other areas in which we believe planning is important. We would never try to build a house without a set of plans. We make business plans and vacation plans. Generals make battle plans, and politicians make campaign plans. Coaches give their players a game plan. Yet for a variety of reasons, ministries, nonprofits, and most individuals place little value on a plan.

For example, I often hear ministry leaders contend that planning is inconsistent with trusting God. Also, leaders tend to be right-brained and value creativity and imagination over planning. Sometimes planning is bypassed simply because it's hard work and not as glamorous as the actual endeavor of achieving a vision. Then there's confusion about what a plan really is that prevents leaders from developing one. The worst reason I've heard more than once is that planning is not biblical. Leaders fall back on, "Just let go and let God." I tried that once. My wife is still laughing. As far as I'm concerned, these are just excuses for not wanting or not being able to develop a simple, credible, and sequential plan that will successfully turn a dream into a reality.

Some of the resistance to planning may be due to the fact that people tend to resist accountability. You can fire people up with your vision, but if you don't have a plan, no one can hold you accountable. A well thought-out and credible plan can be reviewed, letting people know exactly how you are progressing toward your vision. That can be uncomfortable.

PLANNING IS BIBLICAL

When David cast his vision for building the Temple, he included the fact that he had a plan to execute that vision: "I had it in my heart to build a house as a place of rest for the Ark . . . and I made plans to build it" (1 Chronicles 28:2). David conveyed his vision and his plan. It was not only in the same sentence, but in the first sentence. He understood that visions and plans are inseparable. I have never been approached by a ministry seeking my support where in the same breath they shared their dream and the existence of a plan. Never. This often-overlooked phrase may be the most important message in the entire story of the building of the Temple: "I made plans." David's vision would have remained an empty dream if he had not been willing to think through every detail required to accomplish this significant goal. Compelling models of planning are woven throughout the Bible. This should not surprise us. Experience shows that planning dramatically increases the probability of achieving a vision.

The biblical models of planning start in Genesis and paint a striking picture of how important it is. After he was sold into slavery, Joseph revealed the importance of planning in order to accomplish a dream. The Pharaoh had been troubled by dreams that he was unable to interpret. Because of his gifts and God's intervention, Joseph not only explained what the dreams meant (seven years of good harvests followed by seven years of severe drought and famine), but he also described a detailed plan for how to respond to the situation.

His plan included the appointing of appropriate leadership, the specific percentage of stockpiling, the location for those stockpiles, and their security. As the years of famine arrived and intensified, his plan for disseminating grain was ready, sustaining not only Egypt but saving Joseph's Hebrew family as well.

Nearly four hundred years later, as Joseph's people made their way back to Canaan, the Bible records another detailed plan for a place of worship, the precursor to the Temple David later dreamed of. The Tabernacle was a moveable temple, a center-piece for the worship and life of the Israelites as they wandered in the desert after being freed from slavery. Moses received the specific plan as he spent time with God. The details of the plan are recorded in fifteen consecutive chapters in the book of Exodus. They include a strategy for gathering resources from the community, lists of the raw materials needed, the physical

design and ornamentation for key objects, the exact measure-
ments of the space and precisely how it was to be divided, the
colors for the cloth, the pattern for the priests' clothing and
ceremonial items, specific precious stones to be used, and the
words that were to be engraved on them. Even the individual
craftsmen who were to oversee specialized teams were named.
The extensive precision is almost overwhelming.

Almost five hundred years after the construction of the
Tabernacle, David began his planning for the permanent
Temple, as recorded in 1 Chronicles 28:11-18.

Throughout the Bible, there are many more references
to planning. The New Testament book of Matthew continually points out how Jesus' birth, life, death, and resur-
rection were according to the plans God had laid out all
through the Old Testament and from eternity past. Perhaps
it is from this grand plan that we sometimes refer to "the
plan of salvation." The book of Acts shows the Apostle Paul
collaborating with the Holy Spirit on the plans for each of
his missionary travels. In the English translation, the third
chapter of Paul's letter to the Ephesians uses the word *plan*
five times, describing God's step-by-step, specific intentions
for taking the good news to the Gentiles.

Joseph, Moses, David, and the Apostle Paul are but a handful of human examples from Scripture about the necessity of planning. These and others follow the pattern set out by their Maker, for God is clearly planning His handling of history from the beginning. Proverbs is replete with wisdom about planning, telling us not to plot harm but to be righteous in our preparation, to gather wise counsel, and to commit our plans to the Lord.

Proverbs also reminds us that while God ultimately determines the outcome of our plans, He desires that we be diligent in designing them. He has a plan for one of his more remarkable creations: *you*. And it's a good plan, as we learn in Jeremiah 29:11: "For I know the plans I have for you . . . plans to prosper you and not to harm you, plans to give you a future and a hope." If God plans and if planning is lifted high in Scripture as "a future and a hope," it should be something we take seriously as well. People pursuing a dream without a plan do so at their peril.

THE BENEFITS OF PLANNING

All of these biblical models and admonitions underscore an important truth. The hard work of planning dramatically increases the probability of achieving a dream or vision. Or as Solomon once wrote, "Good planning and hard work lead to prosperity, but hasty shortcuts lead to poverty" (Proverbs 21:5). There are many reasons for this relationship of success between planning and accomplishment. Here are just a few of the ways a detailed plan can increase the chance of significant achievement.

Recognizes Potential Obstacles

Developing a plan ahead of time and then working through it will help you identify the challenges that can derail your dream. We sometimes refer to these as contingency plans, meaning we identify what might go wrong and what we will do if it does.

Identifies the Wisest Path

Without a plan, when you encounter an obstacle or glitch on your way toward accomplishing your vision, you have to make a hasty decision. If you have a plan, you are able to see those obstacles in advance and choose the best way to get to your destination. For example, there may be three right ways to achieve your vision, but what's the *best* one of the three for you?

Enhances Focus

Keeping first things first is the only way to discern mere distractions from true opportunities or emergencies. With any major endeavor, you will encounter new ideas, possible shortcuts, and countless "Why don't we do this?" suggestions from well-meaning colleagues. A plan focused on priorities guards against the tyranny of the urgent. It also helps you know when to say no to apparent new opportunities.

Prepares Hearts and Minds

When you create a plan and share it with those who will help you implement it, you are communicating an important message to them: "You play a valuable role in our vision." One of the key challenges to any organization is stewarding morale. Communicating your plan builds the morale of everyone in the organization. Perhaps that is one of the reasons the people of Israel so joyfully gave to the Temple-building project—they knew the plan. A credible plan lets everyone involved know exactly what to expect as they all do their part in achieving your organization's vision.

Identifies Resources

What would it take to build the Temple? David made it painstakingly clear. Just read his list in 1 Chronicles 28:11-18. The Israelites knew exactly what was needed. A great plan reveals the resources, skills, talents, and time you will need to achieve your vision. Why launch into something if you don't really know what it will require?

Defines Responsibilities

Football coaches spend a great deal of time developing a "game plan" that identifies what each of the twenty-two players on offense and defense are expected to do. No coach would send his players on to the field relying on words and no plan. So why would you challenge your organization to go out and accomplish something meaningful without making sure every person knows what to do? When boundaries and roles are clearly in place, everyone knows their task and can be held accountable for carrying it out. In practical terms, a plan helps avoid conversations filled with comments such as, "I thought *you* were going to do that."

Coordinates Movement

A credible, thorough plan can keep a wide range of parts and people moving in the same direction from beginning to end. Few things sabotage morale more than having people sitting around with nothing to do. When you do not have a plan, that can happen. I've had some experience with building and know what happens when you don't have a plan. The plumbers have to wait because the carpenters haven't framed in the walls, and the electricians have to wait until the plumbing is completed before they can run wire.

What army would go to battle without a plan? What building would be built without a plan? What space shuttle would be launched and returned safely to earth without a plan? What real estate developer would purchase acres of land without a plan? Surely, those who seek to serve God would never try to achieve their visions without a plan. Success in any endeavor can never be guaranteed, but planning dramatically increases the probability of seeing your dream become reality. There is no substitute for planning. It is indispensable!

THREE QUESTIONS TO ASK ABOUT A CREDIBLE PLAN

Deciding you need a plan is one thing—and I hope I've convinced you that moving forward without a plan is sheer folly. But how do you actually put together a plan? It isn't glamorous. Essentially, it's the work of mapping out how to get from where you are to where your vision calls you. And while it is beyond the scope of this short book to explain the entire planning process, a credible plan contains three essential elements: it should be written, it should be measurable, and it should be responsive to the unexpected.

Is it written down?

As a young man, I was asked by a wise business leader where my plan was for a business idea. I smugly pointed to my head. He said, "A plan that is not in writing is not a plan." It was a vital lesson to learn at a young age.

Why does a plan need to be in writing? First, when you have something written down on paper—even if it is a very rough draft—it is easier to ask the counsel of others, something that is essential to developing a credible plan. Yes, you could verbally share your plan with a trusted advisor, but people generally only retain about seventeen percent of what they hear. Second, a written plan increases the chances that those who support you will know exactly what is expected of them. My wife learned this long ago. Verbally conveying the Saturday chore plan to our kids often resulted in confusion and arguing. A written Saturday plan put everyone on the same page (literally). Finally, writing well requires thinking well, and the writing process itself necessitates the critical thinking essential for a credible plan.

Don't just take my word for it. In 1 Chronicles 28:19, David told Solomon that "every part of the plan" for the Temple "was written under the direction of the LORD." Notice he specifically said *every part* was *written*. As we have seen already, written plans are evident throughout the Bible. God gave specific instructions and preparation to the Old Testament prophets, telling them explicitly to write them down. Many New Testament epistles have detailed principles, commands, and expectations for how believers ought to behave and interact with the world, for how the church should be governed, ordered, and understood. It is highly unlikely that the wisdom and instruction contained in these letters would have been transferred and acted on for two thousand years if they had not been written down. Surprisingly, many Christians treasure the written word of Scripture, but resist making a written plan as endorsed or exemplified by the same Scripture!

Can you measure your progress?

Measurement allows us to stay in touch with reality in order to know where we are in relation to the goal. Whether your dream is to build airplanes or love orphans, your plan should set benchmarks to measure at least five categories: what, who, where, when, and how much? Know the materials needed, their quantity, and cost. Know the people who can help you and the skills they bring to match the tasks. Set goals for where you need to be, both geographically and on your timeline.

Another reason to have a measurable plan is that it allows the leader to hold other parties responsible for their part in accomplishing the vision. Like the Saturday work plan in our home where each of the kids knew his or her role in getting things done, we knew exactly whom to talk to when the trash was neglected or a room had not been dusted.

Can you respond to the unexpected?

The Apostle James, in his letter to the twelve scattered tribes, underscores the need for our plans to be flexible:

> Now listen, you who say, "Today or tomorrow we will go to this or that city, spend a year there, carry on business and make money." Why, you do not even know what will happen tomorrow . . . You are a mist that appears for a little while and then vanishes. Instead, you ought to say, "If it is the Lord's will, we will live and do this or that." (James 4:13-15)

No plan should be set in stone. It should have the ability to adjust to changing circumstances or unforeseen realities that are bound to come your way. The best way to build responsiveness into a plan is to commit to reviewing it regularly and often. As you review the plan, take action based on what you discover. Military planner Helmuth Von Motke recognized that "no plan survives contact with the enemy." But you don't have to be at war to know that the path to accomplishing a dream can be strewn with sudden unexpected obstacles. A responsive plan is thorough and intentional, but it stays open to God's will and new facts or unforeseen circumstances. Regularly reviewing your plan and keeping it current is the best way to prepare for the unexpected.

CHALLENGES TO PLANNING

To borrow a phrase from a friend of mine, "Planning is simple, but it isn't easy." In other words, there's no magic to creating a plan, just a lot of hard, detail-oriented work. Visionary leaders tend to be right-brain thinkers—creative, risk-taking adventurers. Planning leans more to the left side of the brain because it is analytical and logical. While dreaming is often energizing, writing a credible plan can be tiring for the right-brained leader. Consequently, it seems almost anticlimactic after the rush of getting the vision.

Creating a written plan might also feel daunting if relentless attention to detail is not your gift. Visionaries who are energized by the dreaming process sometimes pause at the planning step simply because working at the required level of specifics is not their area of strength. If this describes you, accept it as quickly as possible. Then find the right partner or advisor whose strength is planning.

A lack of expertise is often a further challenge to planning, and involving others is the solution. No one is an expert on every topic, yet discouragement tempts us when we run into our own inexperience with a subject or the planning process itself. Even master architect I.M. Pei, winner of the Pritzker Prize (the Nobel Prize for architecture), is not an expert on all the sub-systems in a project. Consequently, he cannot complete his building plans without relying on mechanical or electrical engineers for their expertise. Don't hesitate to ask for help from someone you respect.

The final challenge is that planning can be overwhelming. As you begin to see how much is involved, it may feel like dumping a two-thousand-piece jigsaw puzzle on a table. Looking at too many pieces all at once has a tendency to paralyze. If you identify with this idea, consider the way climbers ascend Mt. Everest. The route to the peak has multiple base camps. You could break up your vision into multiple base camps. Then develop a comprehensive, detailed plan to reach each one. As you approach one camp, you can identify and develop the plan to reach the next and so on. I have to remind myself constantly to take the planning process one step at a time.

The challenges of planning effectively are significant, but planning is biblical, and it dramatically increases the chance of success. As you write a measurable, responsive plan, you may face hard work, countless details, or your own lack of expertise. Finding wise partners and insightful allies makes a big difference. Look for individuals whose gifts complement yours. If you are creative, enlist someone who is left-brained. Bankers, physicians, scientists, lawyers, accountants, business executives, and operating officers are good choices. There are few challenges that can't be made smoother by assembling a good team that works together for the same goal.

Another biblical story of planning focuses on Nehemiah. Solomon completed the Temple in Jerusalem around 960 B.C. Generations of kings came and went after him with less and less commitment to leading with integrity. Eventually, by 446 B.C., foreign invaders had overrun Israel, and most of its people lived in exile in Persia under the rule of King Artaxerxes. Nehemiah, an Israeli refugee, held a special position in the king's court. In the fall of that year, Nehemiah learned that "the wall of Jerusalem has been torn down, and the gates have been burned" (Nehemiah 1:3). The city where his ancestors were buried was in ruins. Nehemiah passionately desired to return and rebuild the city of Jerusalem. With so much at stake, he had to invest in a credible plan.

After months of prayer and planning, Nehemiah risked his life by petitioning the king for the right to pursue a personal dream. He was well prepared for Artaxerxes's questions. "*What* is it you want?" (Nehemiah 2:4) was followed promptly with, "*How* long will your journey take?" and,

"*When* will you get back?" (Nehemiah 2:6). Nehemiah was ready with specific answers, showing his planning and foresight. Nehemiah took a bold step. He asked for and secured letters to the governors of Trans-Euphrates for permission to travel through their land. He even requested a letter to the manager of the king's forest, asking for timber needed to rebuild walls and gates. Nehemiah was then prepared to meet with the governors and set out for Jerusalem.

Upon arrival, he kept his purpose and plan to himself while he began gathering additional facts, securing some information even in the dead of night. He went on to articulate his vision formally, and then to implement his plan, assigning detailed responsibilities, locating various work forces, and executing strategy to defend against hostile forces.

The time spent planning was well rewarded. The workers completed the rebuilding of the wall and the gates in just fifty-two days. The reactions to this accomplishment were effectively summarized in Nehemiah 6:15: "When our enemies heard about this, all the surrounding nations were afraid and lost their self-confidence because they realized that this work had been done with the help of our God."

SAMPLE ACTION PLAN

Vision:_____

Step	Person	Date / Deadline	Cost	Action
1.	Wendy	Oct 2012	$5,000	Prepare verbal and written materials for donor presentations
2.	David	Jan 2013	$15,000	Secure new major donors. Goal: $400,000
3.	Wendy	Feb 2013	$50,000	Secure Marketing firm
4.	Mary	Apr 2013	$15,000	Complete Spanish translation of curriculum
5.	Marketing	Apr 2013	$60,000	Contract with IT Firm
6.	David	Oct 2013	$30,000	Hold annual fundraising events
7.	David	Jul 2014	$10,000	Secure initial capital for Field Directors in target markets. $300,000
8.	David	Oct 2014	$300,000	Hire two Field Directors in target cities
9.	David	Oct 2014	$30,000	Hold annual fundraising events

SUMMARY

CHAPTER 4 – DEVELOPING A CREDIBLE PLAN

PLANNING IS BIBLICAL

THE BENEFITS OF PLANNING
  Recognizes Potential Obstacles
  Identifies the Wisest Path
  Enhances Focus
  Prepares Hearts and Minds
  Identifies Resources
  Defines Responsibilities
  Coordinates Movement

THE THREE ELEMENTS OF A CREDIBLE PLAN
  Written
  Measurable
  Responsive

CHALLENGES TO PLANNING
  Hard Work
  Lack of Expertise
  Feeling Overwhelmed

BREAKTHROUGH

CHAPTER FIVE

SELECTING THE RIGHT LEADER

*"Give me wisdom and knowl-
edge, that I may lead this people."*
2 Chronicles 1:10

"Wisdom is the right use of knowledge."
Charles Haddon Spurgeon

L EADERSHIP IS BIG business. Google the term *leadership
seminars* and thirty-two million choices await you.
Type the phrase *leadership books* into Amazon's search
function, and at last count, more than ninety-two thousand
titles appear. When I began my career I had never heard of
an *executive coach*. Today, it is not uncommon for a leader
to have his or her own coach to help navigate the challenges
of leadership. And if you still need more advice on how to

lead, you can subscribe to *CEO Journal, Chief Executive,* or *Leadership Excellence* magazines. Or for leaders of Christian organizations, *Leadership Journal* is available.

With all these excellent resources for leaders, what could an ancient text—the Old Testament—add to the vitally important topic of leadership? Plenty.

While I certainly have not read every book on leadership or attended every seminar, most of what I see on this topic focuses on strategies, styles, methods, or techniques. In other words, leadership is a skill, and to be a better leader, you just need to learn the right skills and implement them as you lead your organization. Although skills are important, they miss the essence of leadership, and that's where Solomon comes in. His approach, as recorded in the Old Testament story of building the Temple, provides the necessary ingredient to leadership that not only helps turn dreams into reality, but also offers powerful potential wisdom and knowledge, for *any* situation.

Whether you lead a Fortune 500 company, your own small business, a nonprofit organization, a faith-based ministry, or even your family, the foundations of effective leadership are wisdom and knowledge. They long precede any skill set, and they come from the very core of who you are. Styles, techniques, methods, and skills are important, but without the right foundations, they will not be enough. In other words, you can have all the right skills and still be an ineffective leader if you lack wisdom and knowledge.

Solomon was considered the wisest man ever to live. Who could possibly measure up to his standards of wisdom and knowledge? If perfection is your goal, then yes, it will be impossible to measure up. But I've always believed in aiming high. You may not reach the top, but by striving for it, you'll get a lot higher than you would have if you settled for mediocrity.

Also, keep in mind that neither David nor Solomon was a perfect leader. David's failure prevented him from building the Temple, and later in life Solomon veered off course, never to accomplish anything significant thereafter. Your goal in leadership is not perfection. Yet by setting your sights high, you will stretch and grow into the best possible leader you can be.

ASK AND YOU SHALL RECEIVE

The Harvard Business Review conducted a survey of young leaders, asking what they wanted most. The answers were wide-ranging and extraordinary. More than ninety percent said they wanted "diversity in the workplace." Sixty-four percent said they valued "environmental sustainability." The majority of these young leaders also see mobile technology as the secret to their success. All of these items will give these young leaders an advantage as they step into leadership roles as tomorrow's CEOs and entrepreneurs, but it won't be enough without knowledge and wisdom.

David had an inspiring vision and a credible plan to build a Temple, but he needed the right leader. He had wanted to lead the effort to build a Temple himself, but God chose Solomon instead. After Solomon was appointed king, but before he began constructing the Temple, God invited Solomon to ask God for whatever he wanted.

Put yourself in Solomon's sandals for a minute. Suppose God is asking you that same question regarding your vision. What would you ask for? More money? In my experience, that's often the case. More and better people working for you? More time? More control and authority over your organization? More respect from those who report to you? A new board? A miracle?

Solomon did not hesitate to answer. He knew the task before him would require immense resources, but he did not ask for money. He knew the building of the Temple would take a long time, but he did not ask for a long life so that he could see the fruits of his leadership. None of these requests would have been out of order, but he answered, "Give me *wisdom* and *knowledge* that I may *lead* these people, for who is able to govern these great people of yours" (2 Chronicles 1:10 [emphasis added]).

Solomon's response apparently pleased God:

> Since this is your heart's desire and you have not asked for wealth, riches or honor, nor for the death of your enemies, and since you have not asked for a long life but for wisdom and knowledge to govern my people over whom I have made you king, therefore wisdom and knowledge will be given to you. And I will also give you wealth, riches, and honor, such as no king who was before you ever had and none after you will have. (2 Chronicles 1:11-12)

Imagine what might happen if instead of asking God to help you raise enough money to accomplish your goals, you asked him for knowledge and wisdom *in order to lead effectively.* Apparently these two components of leadership are more important to God than anything else—so much so that he rewarded Solomon additionally with "wealth, riches, and honor." Because knowledge and wisdom are so important to God, take a closer look at what they are and how they impact the life of a leader.

KNOWLEDGE

Obviously, leaders need to know a lot in order to accomplish their goals and dreams. Knowledge generally refers to the cognitive or mental process and includes such things as "facts, information, and skills acquired through experience or education."[4] In general terms, this means that a leader should always be learning. Earning a college or advanced degree is never enough. But what exactly should you be learning? Two major categories of leadership come to mind: knowledge of relevant facts and knowledge of truth.

Facts

It stands to reason that you can't lead a relief and development organization if you don't know much about relief and development. Similarly, if you've been trained as an engineer but feel called to lead an inner-city mission, you'll need to gain knowledge of things like substance abuse, job training, and community development. Every organization or individual operates with a specific knowledge base. It is important for leaders to know relevant information about the specific area in which they lead, especially when leading others to realize a dream. One of Solomon's own Proverbs states that it is "both foolish and shameful" to respond to a situation without knowing "the facts" (Proverbs 18:13, NLT).

In today's world, we place a high value on a college degree, and I generally endorse that choice. But there are other effective ways to gain knowledge. Just look at the list of successful people who never earned a college degree: Bill Gates of Microsoft, Mark Zuckerberg of Facebook, and from previous generations, Andrew Carnegie, Winston Churchill, Walt Disney, and John D. Rockefeller. You might say these people earned their degrees in the "school of life," which can be a great way to supplement your own formal education. How? Become a lifelong learner. Never be satisfied with what you know. The late Peter Drucker disciplined himself to study a new subject every three years. Independent reading and study not only help you acquire information about a subject, but also keep your mind active and alert. College is important, but what's even more important is developing a mindset of learning that will serve you well as a leader.

Leaders also gain knowledge by listening. Knowledge of important facts can come from almost anyone to whom we are willing to give our full attention. Parents, bosses, boards of directors, and even strangers who have firsthand experience with our area of leadership can become a valuable source of relevant facts and information. During the 1980s, the phrase "management by wandering around" was coined to describe a style of leadership based on getting out of the office and walking around your company. This is an excellent way for an executive to lead a company more effectively. It's amazing what you can learn by listening to those around you.

Knowledge of facts is also essential to decision making. Immediately after his watershed request for wisdom and knowledge, Solomon used his knowledge of the facts to make a very difficult decision. Approached by two women who both claimed to be the mother of a baby, Solomon listened carefully to the details of their story. Before making any judgment, he essentially wanted to get the facts straight (1 Kings 3:16-28).

Leaders who want to accomplish their dreams and goals face a continuous barrage of tough decisions. You can have great skills and know all the right techniques for leading an organization, but if you do not have knowledge of the pertinent facts, you will eventually fail as a leader. However, knowledge of facts is not enough. One must also have knowledge of truth.

Truth

Truth, by definition, is absolute. Unfortunately, we live in an era where many voices claim there is no absolute truth. "Truth is relative, so you need to find *your* truth," some say. "I will find *my* truth, and then we will all get along fine," claim others. A godly leader recognizes the folly of this kind of thinking. He knows that truth is absolute, and its foundation rests in the Bible in time-tested, unchanging principles. Consider, for example, the Ten Commandments, a concise yet powerful expression of truth. Don't cover up or fail to be transparent, even if it means admitting you made a mistake. Don't take what doesn't belong to you. Don't worship anyone or anything but God. Don't covet your colleague's office. You get the idea. These commandments provide focus for leadership and establish a standard of personal conduct and societal justice. Interestingly, many of these principles show up in other places such as Hammurabi's Code, the writings of Cicero and Aristotle, the Koran, even Norse traditions.

Solomon's deep understanding of these ten truths provided inestimable value for him. They eliminated distractions and expedited his decisions. As he considered the two women in his court, he understood that the false mother had violated several commandments by coveting the other woman's child, stealing, lying, and ultimately being willing to murder the baby. Guided by his knowledge of these unchanging principles, Solomon effectively resolved the conflict.

Knowledge of the facts, character, and truth is the foundation for leadership. The person who prioritizes the lifelong pursuit of this kind of knowledge has the makings of a great leader, the kind of leader who can successfully turn a dream into reality. Solomon probably said it best when he wrote,

"Wise people treasure knowledge" (Proverbs 10:14, NLT). But for the right leader, knowledge is only the beginning.

WISDOM

Have you known individuals who are smart, but do not appear wise? They know a lot of facts, have access to helpful data and research, yet when it comes to applying all that they have learned, they falter. Why? Because they lack wisdom, which is expressed by applying knowledge to their personal character and making wise decisions.

A friend recently told me about a very bright young man in his company who was promoted to a position of leadership in one of the departments. This man had two Ph.D.s and knew a great deal about many things. Yet he struggled in his new position. He had difficulty making decisions and motivating his team. He was such a bad fit that he eventually asked to be demoted to his original position (which actually demonstrated some wisdom and strong character on his part). As my friend summarized, the man had all the knowledge but did not know how to use it effectively as a leader.

The Book of Proverbs makes a very simple case for wisdom: "Wisdom is supreme; therefore get wisdom" (Proverbs 4:7). But how exactly do you *get* wisdom? If we pay attention to this book of wisdom, we will discover direction and examples of how to obtain it:

- "Hold on to instruction, do not let it go . . . " (Proverbs 4:13).

- "Listen to my instruction and be wise." (Proverbs 8:33)

- " . . . with humility comes wisdom." (Proverbs 11:2)

- "He who walks with the wise grows wise . . . " (Proverbs 13:20).

From these and other admonitions, we gain wisdom by applying God's instruction to our hearts and allowing that instruction to influence our behaviors and decisions. That is what builds character. But perhaps the best summary of all of these paths to wisdom—and its offspring, character—is summed up in these words: "The fear of the Lord is the beginning of wisdom" (Proverbs 9:10). In other words, wisdom starts with submission to God's authority. It sounds simple enough but is not always practiced, even in the church.

Character

Increasingly in today's world, a leader must also commit to understanding the vital place of personal character, both for himself and for those he leads. Journalist and longtime political observer Gail Sheehy says that while character is the most crucial element of leadership, it is also the most elusive.[5] A recent *Forbes* magazine article listed fifteen ways to identify bad leaders. Second on their list: character. "A leader who lacks integrity or character will never stand the test of time."[6] To be worthy of leadership and to lead effectively, one must be able to demonstrate character and evaluate it in others.

What do I mean by character? Various definitions refer to those qualities that make up and distinguish an individual. I'm referring here to traits such as honesty, integrity, fairness, and morality. In other words, a leader with character will do the right thing regardless of the circumstances or outcomes, and he will recruit those who do the same.

Throughout his Proverbs, Solomon describes the benefits of virtuous character. But he also lived out these admonitions as he led the building of the Temple. Great leaders know the difference between right and wrong and place a priority on always doing the right thing. As I noted earlier, Solomon ultimately failed in the character department. His successes came when he obeyed God without wavering.

This view of applied wisdom is compatible with the way William Whewill, an influential nineteenth-century British scientist and philosopher, described it: "knowing the right thing to do and doing it the right way." In other words, wisdom seems to be most clearly revealed in taking what we know (knowledge) and making right decisions with it.

Wise Decision Making

We all make countless decisions daily. We decide to act on or ignore facts, to engage in or avoid good character, to accept or reject truths. Even the choice to not decide is a decision. Ultimately, the sum of a leader's decisions allows a dream to succeed or dooms it to failure. Both David's and Solomon's lives illustrated that a leader's wisdom, or lack thereof, will generally be revealed in his decision making. I have found the proving ground of wisdom seems to be most often encountered in decisions in at least four areas: setting priorities, staying focused, selecting people, and sustaining performance.

Setting Priorities

You've likely heard of the phrase "the tyranny of the urgent." It refers to the perpetual competition for what needs attention on the way to achieving any dream. A wise leader recognizes the need to establish priorities so that he isn't continually reacting to the latest crisis (flexibility in the plan). Leaders are inundated with choices about what needs their focus. Failed presidencies, projects, and partnerships often result from the inability to set priorities or the selection of the wrong ones. Wisdom requires one to draw on knowledge to choose what is worth doing first. President Ronald Reagan was a master of the following precept: "The President should do what only he can do. Everything else, somebody else." On the other hand, President Lyndon Johnson destroyed his presidency by micromanaging everything, including selecting targets for airstrikes in Vietnam.

Conceivably, priorities can be based on any criteria, including the leader's ego or success at any cost. Wisdom involves choosing "the right things" to focus upon. Knowledge of facts, character, and truth are critical in setting priorities. They act as a keel to keep your organization focused on the right things. Solomon set a priority to build the Temple before building his own palace (1 Kings 6-7). In doing so, the young king revealed his dedication to the pursuit of the right priorities.

Staying Focused

In my experience, the two biggest impediments to dreams being realized are the lack of planning and the failure to stay focused. It doesn't matter if it's a CEO of a publicly traded company or an individual just starting out in a career. The two go hand in hand. I have a plan, and I must stay focused on it. Leadership that is unfocused usually produces chaos within the organization. Conversely, one of the most important, practical, and relevant demonstrations of wisdom is the discipline of staying focused.

Lack of focus tends to be more prevalent in the dynamic, creative leader, who often grows weary of the present and is always looking for the next big project or challenge. I've also seen this in competent leaders whose compassion calls them to respond to each heart-rending crisis. These leaders are often charismatic and impressive, yet they find it hard to stay focused on a single vision or dream.

Lack of focus manifests itself in many ways: inefficiencies, mission drift, organizational chaos, employee turnover, and cost overruns. Unfortunately, these are all-too-common occurrences in Christian ministries. Sometimes leaders are unable to pinpoint the source of the problem. Sometimes they blame these problems on the wrong issue. However, the real culprit is often a lack of focus.

Once again, Solomon's example offers us clues to the challenge of staying focused. Immediately after God answered Solomon's prayer for wisdom and knowledge, the Bible says, "Then Solomon returned to Jerusalem and then built up a huge military force" (2 Chronicles 1:13-14, NLT). This priority was a logical first focus for Solomon, since significant rebellion marked his transition to power. After this was accomplished, "Solomon now decided that the time had come to build a Temple" (2 Chronicles 2:1, NLT). The words "now decided" are also important. They suggest a conscious decision-making process that led to a new focus. Solomon's focus for the next seven years was to build the Temple.

After completing the Temple, Solomon chose a new focus: "Solomon also built a palace for himself and took thirteen years to complete the construction" (1 Kings 7:1, NLT). Seven years to build the Temple, then thirteen years to build the palace.

Only after building his royal palace did Solomon again choose a new focus: "Solomon now turned his attention to rebuilding the towns that King Hiram had given him, and he settled the Israelites in them" (2 Chronicles 8:2). I love the phrase, "now turned his attention to." Once again, there was a conscious decision to keep his attention on one major item at a time. Staying focused is both biblical and powerful. If it enabled Solomon to accomplish all that he did, imagine how it might drastically improve your ability to achieve your dreams.

I suspect all leaders would benefit by following Solomon's example, restricting themselves to one major focus at a time. After understanding Solomon's story, I have committed to do exactly that.

Selecting People

The leader's selection of people also requires wisdom. We are only as good as the company we keep, or as Proverbs put it, "He who walks with the wise grows wise" (Proverbs 13:20). A leader with any experience will quickly realize his ability to accomplish a dream depends upon his wise selection of teammates and followers. In fact, significant research shows that great leaders make a high priority of surrounding themselves with the *right* people.

Solomon seemed to understand this priority. In fact, the Bible indicates Solomon gave first priority to personnel decisions. As Jim Collins suggests in the book *Good to Great,* one of the critical priorities of leadership is "to make sure you have the right people on the bus." Solomon made at least five critical personnel changes immediately after becoming the king of Israel (1 Kings 1:23-46). Issues related to character influenced each of them. Talent is the easy part. Selecting people with character requires wisdom and discernment. Solomon also demonstrated the importance of selecting people when he began building the Temple. He used his knowledge to wisely hire a man named Hiram who was "filled with wisdom, with understanding, and with knowledge to do all kinds of bronze work" for the Temple (1 Kings 7:14). Solomon exhibited wisdom in placing this talented, diligent, and loyal craftsman on his team.

Sustaining Performance

Setting priorities and selecting people tend to be the upfront decisions of leadership. They require the application of wisdom at a specific time. Sustaining daily performance, on the other hand, tests wisdom. It is one thing to pursue your dream with energy and conviction. Maintaining your commitment, however, calls for wise leaders to stay disciplined, focused, and faithful on a daily basis.

Every day can challenge a leader to implement the plan. Wisdom will be needed for each choice along the way. It makes a difference in how a leader aligns his daily conduct to his priorities (founded on knowledge of truth), leverages his people (based on the essentials of good character), and executes his plan (informed by knowledge of the facts). Daily operations can become the point of great risk for leadership failure. To announce belief in certain truths but then act inconsistently when times are tough reveals internal inconsistency and a lack of integrity. Such hypocrisy will push people and their support away.

Solomon knew that "without wise leadership a nation falls" (Proverbs 11:14, NLT), and so do dreams. Knowledge of facts and the essentials of character and truth are valuable, but ultimate power is achieved when men and women use them to make wise decisions. The right leader will prioritize a lifelong pursuit of wisdom that empowers him to set priorities, select people, and sustain performance. Does your dream have the right leader?

PURSUING KNOWLEDGE AND WISDOM

Knowledge and wisdom make up a short list but a tall order. Neither I nor anyone I've met possesses these two qualities fully, but the most influential leaders I know seem to display them in increasing measure over time. In your life's pursuit of wisdom and knowledge, do not underestimate the value of experience.

There is a joke we've heard that is as true as it is humorous: "How do you get good judgment? Experience. How do you get experience? Bad judgment." No matter how much or how little knowledge and wisdom a leader has, he is only one experience away from having more. That's good news, though I would argue that bad judgment is not the only way to gain experience. As the saying goes, "practice makes perfect." You will gain wisdom as you repeatedly practice the process of applying the knowledge of biblical truth to the facts in order to make wise decisions. In an intriguing article, Geoffrey Colvin cites research that suggests the path to greatness is based more on hard work and repetitive practice than on talent. "You will achieve greatness only through an enormous amount of hard work over many years. And not just any hard work, but work of a particular type that's demanding and painful."[7]

That's great news for any of us who think we don't measure up as wise leaders. If we're willing to work at it, we will grow and become wiser with each experience.

Herbert Simon, one of the most influential social scientists of the twentieth century, developed a theory around the rule of ten thousand hours. Practice a musical instrument or a sport for ten thousand hours and during those hours, strive constantly to get better. At the end you will have achieved a world-class mastery of the skill, regardless of the lack of any natural talent at the start. His theory supports the view of a coach who repeatedly said to his athletes, "Hard work beats talent." Similarly, gaining wisdom is simply a matter of making its practice a priority. Meanwhile, the benefit of gaining knowledge and wisdom is felt all along the way, not just at the end of ten thousand hours.

Another way to increase wisdom is to talk with others about their experience, though most of us are reluctant to do this. Instead, we learn the hard way, by our own mistakes. "Plans fail for lack of counsel, but with many advisers they succeed," Solomon wrote (Proverbs 15:22). Listen to people who have followed similar dreams. Ask questions about where they failed and succeeded. Invite their insight and discernment about your current situation. Let the lessons they learned speak into your circumstances. Your knowledge and wisdom will flourish.

KNOWING WHEN TO STEP ASIDE

One final, and possibly painful, word on leadership. One of the characteristics of a great leader is that he knows when to step aside and helps pave the way for the next leader to be successful. Some businesses and organizations suffer from a disease I call *founderitis*. They began under the visionary leadership of a founder, but then plateau or flounder when it's clear that new leadership is needed. And even if that founder eventually turns the ministry over to someone else, things can go from bad to worse because no one planned for the transition.

David clearly wanted to build the Temple, but he handed the leadership of that grand dream to Solomon. It could have been messy. In today's language, David was "relieved of his responsibilities." As the CEO, he stood in front of his leadership team and said, "God said to me, 'You are not to build a house for my Name'" (1 Chronicles 28:3). We have no record that he argued to hold onto his job or that he left in a huff. Instead, he not only selected Solomon, but warned him about various issues to which he should be alert as he assumed a position of leadership. In addition, David left Solomon an inspiring vision, a credible plan, substantial resources, and a united constituency. In other words, David helped prepare Solomon so the transition would be seamless.

Being the right leader usually is not a lifetime assignment. Effective, wise leadership is difficult, but perhaps the most difficult challenge for any leader is knowing when it's time to pass the baton to someone else. How do you know? In David's charge to Solomon, I believe he offers insight into how anyone finds direction: "acknowledge the God of your father, and serve him with wholehearted devotion and with a willing mind . . ." And then "If you seek him, he will be found by you" (1 Chronicles 28:9).

I've heard it said that some of the best sermons speak to the preacher as much as to the congregation. The same could be said about my comments on wisdom and knowledge. Even as I write this, I am reminded how far short of the ideal my own leadership performance has been. The benefits of wisdom and knowledge that I describe throughout this chapter apply to me, first and foremost, but I hope to you as well.

It Is Not Impossible

Someone recently asked me who I thought "measured up." Three leaders immediately came to mind. Do not think the standards I have outlined in this chapter are impossible to achieve. If you are still doubtful, you can read more about these three leaders in the appendix.

Of course, there are other fine examples of the right leader. They pursue knowledge of facts, character, and truth. And they ask God for wisdom when setting priorities, staying focused, selecting people, and sustaining performance. No matter how difficult the task, they keep reaching for knowledge and wisdom. Who would you put on your list of right leaders?

As a leader or one with influence over others, don't get discouraged. Take the words of Winston Churchill to heart: "Never, never, never, never give up." Solomon seemed to do exactly this, and the Wailing Wall (a remnant of his Temple) still stands as testament to his quest.

BREAKTHROUGH

SUMMARY

CHAPTER 5 – SELECTING THE RIGHT LEADER

KNOWLEDGE
  Facts
  Truth

WISDOM
  Character
  Wise Decision Making
    Setting Priorities
    Staying Focused
    Selecting People
    Sustaining Performance

PURSUING KNOWLEDGE AND WISDOM
  Prioritize the Lifelong Pursuit of Knowledge
  and Wisdom
  Practice Makes Perfect
  Multitude of Counsel

KNOWING WHEN TO STEP ASIDE

BREAKTHROUGH

CHAPTER SIX

SEEKING INITIAL FUNDING

"Then King David said . . . 'I now give my personal trea-
sures of gold and silver for the temple of my God.'"
1 CHRONICLES 29:1,3 (NIV)

"A journey of a thousand miles begins with a single step."
LAU-TSU

ALL TOO OFTEN after identifying a dream or a vision, both individuals and organizations rush to ask for funding from the public. They assume the sooner they make a broad-based appeal, the quicker the funds will arrive. But this is a serious mistake. It is exactly the opposite of what David did.

Instead, he articulated his vision and then got to work on a detailed, written, credible plan. When it became clear that he was not the leader to fulfill this vision, David chose Solomon, who pursued knowledge and wisdom. With these essentials in place initially, the king of Israel was only then ready to locate funding for the project. And so it will be for you, if you follow the same blueprint God gave to David.

COUNTING THE COST

Before you send out that fundraising letter, take a deep breath and pull out that plan again. At this point, you may not know precisely how much money you'll need, so go through your plan carefully and make honest estimates of how much you believe it will take. If you need help estimating costs, ask someone who knows how to do it. It is vital to do this work if you're going to succeed.

The plan should allow you to identify the cost for each of the steps. It is similar to the process involved in building a house. After the architect creates the plan, an experienced builder will determine the cost for each item. The total is the amount needed to proceed. Even in first-century Palestine, people understood what it meant to identify the cost of a project. Jesus used building costs to make a point about the cost of discipleship. This wisdom applies to fundraising as well: "Suppose one of you wants to build a tower. Won't you first sit down and estimate the cost to see if you have enough money to complete it?" (Luke 14:28). In other words, if you don't accurately estimate the cost of your dream, you could get stuck and end up with an unfinished tower.

Three Steps

While there is a time and place for communicating your financial needs to a wider audience (see the next chapter), doing so prematurely without the benefits of going to a smaller, more intimate audience first is usually counterproductive. You only get one chance to make a good first impression. Don't let impatience or a lack of preparation waste that one opportunity. You lay an important foundation for others when the initial funding comes first from the leader and second from a small cadre close to the leader. Also, if you consider structuring these funds as a matching gift, you can often lay an even better foundation.

Step One: Lead by Example

David made clear that initial funding started with him: "And now, because of my devotion (passion) to the Temple (vision) of my God, I am giving ALL of my own private treasures of gold and silver to help in the construction" (1 Chronicles 29:3, NLT [inserts and emphasis added]). Clearly, David was leading by example.

When David listed all he was going to invest into the building of the Temple, he was demonstrating his own personal belief in the project. This may be one of the reasons the people responded generously. This wasn't a greedy king trying to exploit his minions but a committed, godly leader willing to risk his own wealth before asking anyone else to give.

Not every ministry leader is capable of contributing large sums of money. If your organization is small, and you're living paycheck to paycheck, it might be irresponsible to your family to make a large financial commitment. However, anyone with a big dream should be willing to invest something.

A well-known corporate activist once approached a financier about investing in a takeover bid of an international company. The potential for profit was great. So was the risk. The industrialist was intrigued by the strategist's idea and plan, but he had one question: "How much of your own money are you risking on the deal? If I'm going to put my resources on the line, I need to know you're committed enough to your idea that you'll put your own money there, too." Investors refer to this as having *skin in the game*, and before asking others to give, it is important that leadership convey the level of their commitment in this compelling, tangible way. In other words, if those at the top are unwilling to commit their resources to the dream, why should anyone else?

Step Two: Cultivate a Cadre

After the initial commitment from leadership, it's time for limited, targeted communication with a small group of people who are financially capable of supporting the endeavor. This group of potential supporters should not be selected solely for their money but also for their wisdom. For the leader, this might be the board or some key donors. For the individual, this might be family and close friends. Approaching this small cadre provides a relatively safe arena for practicing your presentation. Even if funds are not secured, this dress rehearsal adds value.

More important, in terms of initial funding, presenting to a few can result in one of three valuable actions:

1) The group invests, and the leader's idea and presentation are validated.

2) The group challenges the vision and plan, which are improved. Then they invest and the leader's idea is validated.

3) The group says no and does not invest, and the leader's vision may require reworking.

The small assembly provides a vital practice field where the leader can improve and refine the vision and the plan.

Step Three: Consider a Matching Gift

The topic of a matching gift is not found in the biblical text. I recommend it based on my experience, logic, and passion for its power.

As you look for initial funding, consider structuring contributions using this well-known but often underutilized strategy that can motivate your initial investors as well as the wider audience of potential supporters. The initial funder benefits because he knows his money will not be used unless other funds are received. When additional funds come in, the initial donor feels encouraged. His or her generosity allows the gift to be a catalyst for new donors. Finally, a matching grant motivates people for whose funds you ask when you go public (see the next chapter, "Going Public"). This applies especially to business donors and those motivated by metrics such as *return on investment*.

Although David's gift was not described as a matching gift, there are some similarities. As mentioned earlier, he gave all his personal gold and silver "to help in the construction" (1 Chronicles 29:3, NLT). Obviously, his own resources were inadequate to achieve his vision (as is the case with most). And only if others helped would the Temple get built. What would have happened to David's gift if he hadn't received the remaining resources?

A matching gift should never be characterized as such unless it truly is one. It should be contingent upon its being matched in accordance with its terms including a specified time period. Sometimes matching gifts are abused by promoting the gift as matching when it is given unconditionally. This is misleading and harmful and could undermine the confidence of the ministry staff. Donors may fail to respond to matching gift offers if they believe they are shams. This is very unfortunate. It would be wonderful if this trend could be reversed — even one ministry at a time.

I recently received a call from the CEO of Biblica (formerly International Bible Society). Founded in 1809, Biblica is responsible for sponsoring and funding the translation of the New International Version of the Bible, one of the most popular English translations of all time. The CEO told me the Biblica board members had just offered a $600,000 matching gift to help launch Biblica towards its next meaningful destination. I have every confidence the leadership of Biblica will secure a match and use the $1,200,000 wisely in pursuit of a transformational method of distributing the Bible text.

I share this story to encourage other ministries and leaders in situations similar to Biblica to consider using the matching grant approach wisely and properly.

Why Does Initial Funding Matter?

Seasoned fundraisers will tell you it's more difficult to garner the first ten percent of financial support than the last ten percent. But raising initial funding yields at least three benefits.

Provides Credibility

Credibility is the quality that allows *other people* to conclude that a vision has enough merit to take a financial risk by investing dollars. Any source of initial funding suggests that someone believed in the vision enough to participate. This action generates confidence in others and triggers additional generosity.

Overcomes the First-One-In Barrier

Physics reminds us that objects at rest tend to stay at rest unless acted on by some outside force. Initial funding creates the energy that overpowers the psychological inertia that makes many people hesitate to donate. It overcomes the resistance people feel to being the first one to make a donation.

Overcoming this barrier also creates energy for the leader and others. Once capital has been committed, the fundraiser is infused with fresh motivation and excitement. This can be contagious to everyone involved in the project.

When I was a youngster, the church I attended raised

money for missions every year. I was always eager to get to church each Sunday during the fundraising campaign to look at the model of an oversized thermometer displaying the progress toward our mission's goal. Once the red line moved past the first few increments on the thermometer, it rose quickly. Initial funding encouraged others to get on board. People like to see progress.

David's initial gift as well as his passion for the building of the Temple exemplifies the power of initial funding. After overcoming the first-one-in barrier, the project was energized, and additional gifts began to flow.

Creates Momentum

In sports, when a team jumps out to an early lead, it's pretty hard to stop them. It's called momentum, which is another physics term. The same law of physics that describes how to overcome inertia also states that objects in motion tend to stay in motion. This is the power of momentum, and with regard to your dream, it is created by initial funding. It is a critical mass that generates enthusiasm, which builds additional enthusiasm. Everyone wants to get on the bandwagon.

Best-selling author John Maxwell says that momentum is worth three staff members, joking that if leaders got rid of the right three staff members they might jump-start momentum. I don't necessarily advocate firing people, but you don't have to pay momentum a salary or benefits. It is its own source of energy.

David's gift created momentum and prompted a group of committed individuals to contribute. When the time was right, David went public. With initial funding in place, the people in the community followed suit. 1 Chronicles 29:7-8 lists the generous offerings that accumulated. People shared their treasures joyfully.

CONCLUSION

The temptation for every leader is to skip the step of securing initial funding. Please resist that temptation, because it is an important part of the reliable blueprint God has given us through David's example. Once you have your initial funding in place, you are in a much better position to take your dream to a larger audience. You've tested the idea with a trusted small group of investors. Your "thermometer" has inched up to encourage others to join a credible vision. But for that anticipated momentum to take place, you need to reach out to a much larger group. It's time to go public.

SUMMARY

CHAPTER 6 – SEEKING INITIAL FUNDING

COUNTING THE COST

Three Steps

Lead by Example

Test Your Presentation

Consider a Matching Gift

Why Does Initial Funding Matter?

Provides Credibility

Overcomes "First-One-In" Barrier

Creates Momentum

BREAKTHROUGH

Chapter Seven

GOING PUBLIC

"David summoned all the officials of Israel to assemble at Jerusalem . . . . 'Now then, who will follow my example? Who is willing to give offerings to the Lord today?'"
1 Chronicles 28:1, 29:5

"If you want to get in touch with your feelings, fine, talk to yourself. We all do. But if you want to communicate with another thinking human being, get in touch with your thoughts."
William Safire

D AVID TOOK HIS dream, wrote a plan, identified the right leader, and then secured the initial funding for the Temple. With this solid foundation in place, he called the assembly together (1 Chronicles 28). He was ready to go public. This was the right time to do so.

Going public is simply taking your vision or dream to a wider audience and inviting them to provide the support you need to realize your dream. Timing may not be everything, but it is extremely important for this step. The right time to go public is *after* (and only *after*) you have laid the same foundation that David did.

One of the most critical and common mistakes that ministries, entrepreneurs, and dreamers make is to seek broad public support before they do the work required (described in the previous chapters). Their enthusiasm or impatience gets in the way of wise strategy.

Skipping the steps that David followed presents at least three problems:

First, you may lose your one chance to make a good first impression. You don't often get do-overs when you ask people to support your dream.

Second, you risk appearing unprofessional. Enthusiasm and passion will not trump inadequate preparation. If you cannot answer questions or demonstrate a comprehensive and intentional approach to achieving your dream, you will look unprofessional and lose the confidence of your potential donors.

Third, you fail to respect your audience. If you go public

before doing the legwork, you're wasting everyone's time. Few things communicate disrespect more than treating others' time and money lightly. If you are unable to provide the basic foundation of a dream, a plan, a leader, and initial funding, you don't have the right to ask for anyone else's hour, let alone their check.

It's tempting to jump the gun and go right to funding. But when you publicly ask for support before preparing carefully, you put your entire vision at risk.

What to Communicate

David's announcement in 1 Chronicles 28 and 29 provides a model for what you should communicate when you go public: a vision that ignites excitement, a plan that builds trust and credibility, leadership that draws loyalty, and initial funding that prompts giving. In other words, when you go public, communicate everything you have created in working through the previous four chapters.

The Vision

I'm not sure when I first heard the phrase *vision casting*, but it's a great concept when it comes to going public. To break through the din and seize the hearts and minds of your potential supporters, begin with what captured your own heart—your vision. You know it has the power to capture others because it has already inspired you to engage in some hard work to get to this point. David's statement communicated the vision with passion ("I had it in my heart") and with clarity ("to build a house . . . for the ark of the covenant of the Lord"). Can you state your vision with passion and clarity in sixteen words or less?

The Plan

Potential donors may become inspired by your vision. They gain trust in you when you can show them *how* you will turn your vision into reality through your plan. However, this is one part of the presentation where less is more. Explain enough of your planning to enable the audience to see the realistic path to an important goal. Then let them know that a full written plan exists. If appropriate, you might even make copies available for possible donors to review. In his presentation, David did not explain every measurement of the Temple, but he presented Solomon with the written plan. Perhaps the people could see how extensive the document was. They could visibly experience the details without knowing them, and they could trust the plan, for David told them, "All this . . . I have in writing from the hand of the Lord upon me" (1 Chronicles 28:19).

Leadership

If you're going to ask for support, your potential donors may want to know something about the leader, including his or her qualifications and experience. When David presented Solomon to the assembly, he announced his son's resume, starting with the most significant credential — God chose him (1 Chronicles 28:6). Then he describes what this leader must do — follow God's commands and be strong (1 Chronicles 28:8-10). Finally, David acknowledges what Solomon lacks — experience (1 Chronicles 29:1). This combination of confidence and transparency opens the door for the audience to extend their loyalty, support, and grace to the one in charge.

Initial Funding

Going public should build on the momentum created through initial funding. Hearing about the generosity of others prompts generosity in us. David's public communication confirms this. As he describes the initial gifts in 1 Chronicles 29:3-5, not only does he express and share his confidence in the vision, he models the action the community is to take— giving. And they respond accordingly.

In the end, it is a bit of an art to transform the vast collection of knowledge and experience from the first four steps into relevant communication as you go public. Once you have determined the content of your message, it is time to consider how to best deliver it.

Messaging Hints

I cannot tell you exactly how to go public. Rather, I'd like to share from the perspective of someone who has been on the receiving end of countless appeals for support. Consider these hints as you decide how best to communicate your vision to a broader audience.

Say It and Write It

There is a long respected axiom that says if you have something important to communicate, do it both verbally and in writing, appealing to both the ear and the eye. I'm amazed at how many Christian ministries who readily acknowledge the extraordinary value of the *written* Word of God often underuse the power of effective and relevant *written* communication. I have received multiple verbal requests for donations but none in writing. When I asked if there was a written summary available, the answer was almost always no.

As mentioned before, research shows that most people remember only about seventeen percent of what they hear. Therefore, most of your listeners will grasp ideas better through reading. Even in a time when both paper and literacy were somewhat limited, King David kept written records. The plan was in writing as was the entire story of the Temple dream, documented for us in 1 and 2 Chronicles. Here are two comments on written tools:

First, if you intend to present a specific project verbally, leave your audience with a written summary of the major points to read and review on their own. This could be an executive summary or its equivalent. Many of Counsel & Capital's clients have been very successful using its written tools.

Second, if your presentation is directed towards an undesignated gift for the organization, it is common to leave a brochure describing your ministry. Unfortunately, many brochures seem to emphasize quantity and not clarity. One ministry leader recently asked me to support his ministry. He was appropriately and understandably passionate about their work. They served the poor in a part of the world deprived of freedom. He shared from his heart for nearly an hour, but I never quite understood exactly what they did. As he left, he handed me a binder. I glanced inside it and saw multiple inserts, various printed materials, and several CDs. The confusing presentation and chaos implied in their brochure eliminated any interest I had in being a donor.

The lesson from this: don't make going public more complicated than it needs to be. Good communication is transparent, succinct, and direct.

Transparent

Transparency means cultivating an environment of honest, open communication within an organization. This is vital to the organization's health. A board and all its committees should model openness and transparency, with prompt and full disclosure, whether to the full board, the board's delegate (the CEO), financial supporters, other members of the organization, or the general public.

When David passed the leadership to Solomon, he made sure the people knew exactly what they were getting.

> Then King David turned to the entire assembly and said, "My son Solomon, whom God has clearly chosen as the next king of Israel, is still young and inexperienced. The work ahead of him is enormous, for the Temple he will build is not for mere mortals, it is for the LORD God himself!" (1 Chronicles 29:1, NLT)

In that one verse, David publicly acknowledged that Solomon was young and inexperienced. Furthermore, the work would be enormous — man attempting something for God — a daunting proposition.

Conventional wisdom suggests you should try to communicate only the good things about your organization, but you actually gain trust when you communicate things that go wrong. Your community of supporters knows their own lives have ups and downs, and they will not be surprised when mistakes occur or problems arise. Sometimes ministry leaders and nonprofit boards try to hide mistakes. Sophisticated donors know every organization has problems. And every vision involves risks.

One of the world's largest investors once told me the length of time it takes him to find the flaws in an opportunity is inversely proportionate to the likelihood he will invest. Organizations can benefit by being swift to share challenges, risks, or problems. They often fear that doing so will turn donors away. In my experience the opposite occurs. Truth and openness attracts people who want to help solve the very risk or problem the leader is afraid to mention.

Succinct

If you read David's entire speech, which is detailed in 1 Chronicles 28 and most of 29, you will find it takes only about three-and-a-half minutes to say out loud. In that time, he made clear that he had:

1. An Inspiring Vision (Chapter Three)

2. A Credible Plan (Chapter Four) that was demonstrated in writing and provided enough detail so it was credible

3. The Right Leader (Chapter Five) by identifying Solomon as that person and supporting him

4. Initial Funding (Chapter Six) by pledging his own fortune

Then he revealed the risks and made a clear, simple request for funds. All of this in three-and-a-half minutes. Not a bad model for a presentation.

And yet, how many times have you sat through a three-and-a-half minute appeal for funds? A typical presentation lasts an hour (or more), is an emotional discussion of the need, lacks any discussion relating to planning, leadership, and initial funding, and is usually filled with "friendraising" (which, when done just before an appeal for funds, might appear insincere). If you need an hour to ask for support, you risk losing your audience. You may retain their eyes, but their brains will have since returned to a project of their own.

Peter Lynch was a famous investor. Some argue he was responsible for the success of Fidelity Investments and for the mutual fund industry in general. Under his leadership, the fund averaged more than a twenty-nine percent annualized return. As of 2003, his fund had the best twenty-year return of any mutual fund in history.

Leaders and corporations needing investors from around the world would go to him for financial support. When one of our companies contacted him for capital, he agreed to meet, but he provided a caveat. "I will give you three minutes to make your presentation. If you can't tell me what you are doing and why in that amount of time, you haven't worked hard enough to deserve my support."

Frankly, I think Peter Lynch offered leaders and for-profit organizations a great service by issuing that stipulation. It forced them closer to the formula David used and further from the typical approach ministry leaders and entrepreneurs rely on when they are trying to raise capital.

In the end, going public is about *mastering the minimum*— sharing the least amount of relevant information it takes to give the most compelling presentation.

Direct

According to a number of sources, including the respected Yankelovich Research firm, the average person can receive up to twenty thousand marketing messages a day. You read that correctly: twenty thousand a day! Taking your vision public to garner financial support raises that number to twenty thousand and one. In other words, there are a lot of voices competing for attention, and yours has to rise above the rest.

The best way to do this is to follow David's example. Upon going public, he spoke directly: "Listen to me, my brothers and my people, I had it in my heart to build a house as a place of rest for the ark of the covenant of the Lord for the footstool of our God, and I made plans to build it" (1 Chronicles

28:2). In other words, David started his presentation with the bottom line, the punch line. He opened by referring to the destination. He knew his audience and he knew they would find this vision compelling. He didn't beat around the bush. Many people raising financial support have a hard time getting to the point. David did not. He grabbed the audience's attention by immediately and succinctly describing his dream.

The second part of direct communication is being clear in what you want. Look at what David said near the end of his short presentation: "Now then, who will follow my example? Who is willing to give offerings to the Lord today?" (1 Chronicles 29:5). So if you want financial support, ask for it. If you want someone to join your quest, say it. If you want them to volunteer, make that point. If you want their prayer support, request it.

DESIGNATED GIFTS AND BUILDING COMMUNITY

Designated Gifts

Almost every ministry we've worked with concentrates on securing undesignated gifts—that is, gifts that simply go to the general fund and not to a specific project or mission. In fact, leaders often go out of their way to avoid asking for designated funds. Given a choice between $100,000 of designated funds and $75,000 of undesignated funds, the vast majority of ministries would probably take the $75,000. This is understandable. Undesignated funds provide the maximum flexibility and control.

However, a great opportunity exists to engage donors by asking for designated gifts. These requests appeal to many donors, especially if they target their individual passion. In addition, they create an extraordinary opportunity to build confidence and ultimately community. If a ministry would tell a donor what they intend to achieve and occasionally thereafter report the good, the bad, and even the ugly, it would increase the knowledge and confidence of the donor. It would also create many opportunities to have substantive conversations with the donor in the future. David asked for funds *designated* for a specific purpose, the building of the Temple.

Building Community

Most ministries and organizations want to connect with their constituents, including creating a special relationship with their current and future donors. Yet not one ministry I know believes they have even remotely achieved this valuable asset. So how do you build community? Great leaders do so by performing well and communicating well.

Whether or not you agree with all that Franklin D. Roosevelt accomplished, most would say he performed well. During his presidency, the United States emerged from the Great Depression and prevailed in World War II. And during his presidency, the U.S. became one of the world's two superpowers.

Not only did President Roosevelt perform well, he communicated well. He won the hearts of many with his fireside chats, "the first media development that facilitated intimate and direct communication between the president and the citizens of the United States."[8]

Warren Buffet is a more current example of how to build community. His performance is legendary. Starting with paper route proceeds, he built a gigantic company, Berkshire Hathaway. When he took control of the company, its stock price was approximately $30 a share. Today, it is worth nearly $200,000 per share. His investment performance is one of the best ever recorded and his personal net worth, almost all of it in the stock of Berkshire Hathaway, is approximately fifty billion dollars.

However, as a public company chief executive officer, he has taken communication to a new level. Buffett writes an extraordinary annual letter. He starts the draft of each annual letter

Going Public

with the salutation, "Dear Doris and Bertie." Doris and Bertie
are his sisters. He drafts with real people whom he trusts and
cares about in the forefront of his mind. He writes as though
most of their assets are invested in Berkshire Hathaway or they've
have been out of the country for the last year and isolated from
what's going on. He wants to bring them up to date, and he does
so as thoroughly as possible. The letters are often twenty pages
or longer. They have meaningful content and are transparent.
He readily admits his mistakes, whether they are by omission
or commission. Every letter includes sharing credit (see chapter
eight). He praises employees who have performed at a high level.
And he shares the good, the bad, and the ugly about his performance. He writes as if reporting to a large partner or even a boss.
In fact, that is the role of all shareholders.

Most public companies' annual meetings are attended by
less than a hundred people and last for two to three hours.
Berkshire Hathaway's annual meetings last three days and are
attended by over thirty thousand people from every continent
in the world.

What about David? The Bible demonstrates that he also
performed and communicated well. David's leadership career
started in his service to King Saul: "Whatever Saul asked
David to do, David did it successfully" (1 Samuel 18:5).

After he became king, he brought peace to people who had endured four hundred and forty years of fighting. He led most of the battles himself. He brought the Ark of the Covenant to Jerusalem and left the people with a vision, a plan, a leader, and funding to build a temple such as the world had never seen.

In addition to performing well, he communicated well. As a poet and songwriter, David wrote many of the Psalms. On meaningful occasions, he wrote and taught the people the songs he composed. He danced in ecstasy in front of his people when the Ark was brought to Jerusalem, a form of transparent, self-effacing communication that builds community.

What does this mean for you? Community is attainable. It is a function of performing and communicating. When it comes to communication, an annual report is a great place to start. Most ministries that bother to distribute one include a letter from the CEO that is usually only two or three paragraphs long. This type of letter unintentionally sends a message to the ministry's "owners" that the CEO is either too busy or believes the supporters of the ministry are not important enough to justify the time required to write a complete, thorough, and transparent letter. Further, the rest of the annual report often looks more like a sales brochure than a true effort to provide meaningful information to the "owners."

If you want to build a special relationship with your supporters, consider writing the kind of letter you'd send to a family member. Share what is really happening with your organization—the good, but also the challenges and the mistakes. An annual letter written in this manner will go a long way toward building the community you desire.

CONCLUSION

When the time is right, after you've established the vision and the plan and after the leadership and initial funding are in place, the dream is ready to break the surface and be presented to a wider audience. Through well-crafted verbal and written communication, going public is an attention-grabbing invitation for others to participate in a dream. David's actions led the way. As a result, the family leaders, the leaders of the tribes, and the military leaders "all gave willingly" (1 Chronicles 29:6, NLT). No one needed a high-pressure sales pitch before they gave.

Your presentation will invite people into a community committed to honoring God with its resources. And the result will help turn your dream into a reality that will change people's lives. In some churches, after the offering is taken, the congregation joins in singing an old hymn known as "The Doxology." It is a celebratory moment recognizing that all that we have comes from God, and also gives believers the opportunity to give back to His Kingdom.

When people respond to a need and that need is met, we should celebrate by sharing the credit with those who supported our dreams.

SUMMARY

CHAPTER 7 – GOING PUBLIC

WHAT TO COMMUNICATE
Vision
Plan
Leadership
Initial Funding

MESSAGING HINTS
Say It and Write It
Transparent
Succinct
Direct

TWO LAST THOUGHTS
Designated Gifts
Building Community–Perform and Communicate

BREAKTHROUGH

CHAPTER EIGHT

SHARING CREDIT

"Do nothing out of selfish ambition or vain conceit. Rather, in humility value others above yourselves."

PHILIPPIANS 2:3

"There is no limit to what you can accomplish if you don't care who gets the credit."

RONALD REAGAN

JUST A MAN

In year one hundred sixty-one
A new Caesar was crowned
He took a step to insure that
His feet would stay on ground

Caesar Marcus found a slave
And gave him this sole task:
"Remind me that I'm just a man
Whenever I do bask

Within the adulation of
Both follower and fan
Please quell my pride with these four words
And say 'You're just a man'"

I BEGIN WITH THE first portion of a poem[9] about Marcus Aurelius to underscore a temptation every leader faces. Aurelius was considered the last of the Five Good Emperors and a very important Stoic philosopher. He easily could have let his power and success go to his head. But he was wise enough to enlist the help of a slave to keep him humble.

Turning a dream into reality is hard work. Even if you follow the steps we've borrowed from King David, your journey may feel as if you are climbing a mountain—challenging yet exhilarating as you get closer to your goal. Along the way, however, every leader must guard against allowing the joy of accomplishment to become a source of unhealthy pride.

So the final step in achieving your dream is to share the credit with those who helped you along the way. Most leaders of the organizations I've worked with are very good at doing this, much better than I am. But pride can become one of the greatest threats to your leadership as you pursue your dream. It's so easy to begin believing that what you've gained is the result of your skill as a leader.

When the dream is in process, a prideful visionary can miscalculate the danger of his own ego. This is a recipe for making mistakes, and these mistakes can derail the dream. This same pride can also embitter followers and demolish the very support and enthusiasm needed to achieve the dream.

Dreamers are exposed to this enemy especially as they make progress toward their desired result. "Pride goes before destruction" is a biblical truth worth pondering (Proverbs 16:18). Historians paint General George Custer as a talented and rising star who went from second lieutenant to brigadier general in a mere two years. Prior to his ill-fated defeat at Little Big Horn, he was advised to move his troops to another front. But the general refused, trusting his own instincts, and what was the outcome? Only a single horse survived. If everything you do works, you begin to think you are infallible and therefore do not need to listen to others. Furthermore, the more success you achieve, the more acclaim you receive, the greater the tendency to insulate yourself from truth-tellers.

THE INSIDIOUS NATURE OF PRIDE

The Bible includes another story of a king, one who took sole credit for his glorious kingdom. King Nebuchadnezzar was one of the most influential rulers in the history of Babylon. He lived around 560 B.C. After he conquered Israel, he was particularly proud of himself. Daniel, a Jewish prisoner from Israel, encouraged the king to turn from his pride, warning him that he would go insane and live with the animals if he did not change. However, King Nebuchadnezzar resisted the advice, and one evening when he was walking on the roof of the palace, he said, "I, by my own mighty power, have built this beautiful city as my royal residence and as an expression of my royal splendor" (Daniel 4:30). Upon his words, a voice from heaven declared his punishment would begin. Immediately, he lost his mind and was driven from society.

Excessive pride may not cause you to lose your mind, but it will minimize or undermine your dependence on God and others. That's because pride turns the spotlight back on the individual instead of on God's sovereignty. Pride also encourages many leaders to become autocratic and dictatorial, lowering the morale of colleagues and supporters alike. People may initially follow an arrogant leader, but eventually they become disillusioned, even resentful.

When Hitler first came to power, German citizens welcomed him as the savior of their country, but it wasn't long before this adulation went to his head. His advisors soon learned to tell him only what he wanted to hear, and the respect he enjoyed from his citizens soon turned to fear, even loathing.

Wise, effective leaders understand the insidious nature of pride and diligently guard against it.

HUMILITY: THE ANTIDOTE TO PRIDE

Humility is the opposite of pride, and in Western culture, it is increasingly scarce in our leaders. The word *humility* is derived from the Latin word *humus,* the unpretentious layer of fertile soil that nourishes and sustains healthy plants. To be humble, then, means to be rooted in the reality that we are not sufficient by ourselves. It means to be sustained by the truth that we are not infallible or omnipotent. As Thomas Merton instructed, "Pride makes us artificial and humility makes us real."

It will be exciting to see your dream come true, but to avoid the pitfalls of pride, inoculate yourself with a healthy dose of humility.

King David exhibited true humility. He had worked hard. He'd planned for his vision, established leadership, raised support, and communicated to the assembly. He also realized the

Temple was not about him. First and foremost, he understood what was later captured in the answer to the first question of the Westminster Catechism: "The chief end of man is to glorify God." This truth about the proper power source was etched into David's life. The evidence is all over the Psalms he wrote, including Psalm 50, in which David hears God saying that every resource of the earth is His. He reiterated this theme to the crowd when he announced his vision for a Temple. David may have been king of Israel, but he knew who was boss.

When David gathered the assembly, he explained the steps he had taken toward the dream, but he spent a significant quantity of his speech diverting the focus from himself and giving credit to others. David pointed to the power behind his vision:

> Yours, Oh Lord, is the greatness, the power, the glory, the victory, and the majesty. Everything in the heavens and on Earth is yours, Oh Lord, and this is your kingdom. We adore you as the one who is over all things. Riches in honor come from you alone, for you rule over everything. Power and might are in your hand, and it is at your discretion that people are made great and given strength. But who am I, and who are my people, that we could give anything to you? Everything we have has come from you, and we give you only what you have already given us! (1 Chronicles 29:11, 12, 14)

Even King Nebuchadnezzar eventually recognized and gave credit to the true source of his prior greatness. After seven years of living like an animal in the wilderness, Nebuchadnezzar looked up to heaven. Something had changed inside his heart. Humility — seeing himself as he truly was in all his powerlessness — transformed him. Just as suddenly as he lost it, his sanity returned, and he praised and worshipped God. Nebuchadnezzar's kingdom was restored to him "with even greater honor than before" (Daniel 4:36, NLT). And he went on to acknowledge, "Now I, Nebuchadnezzar, praise and glorify and honor the King of Heaven. All His acts are just and true, and He is able to humble those who are proud" (Daniel 4:37, NLT).

Throughout our history, the leaders who tend to be most highly revered also demonstrate the quality of humility. One of the great leaders was Abraham Lincoln, universally recognized as one of the top three American presidents. Consider this small glimpse into what could have been an opportunity for prideful behavior:

> When General Ulysses S. Grant arrived in Washington in 1864 to take command of all the Union armies, a White House reception welcomed him as a conquering hero while Lincoln stood to one side, ceding the place of honor he would normally have occupied. At one point Grant took several strategic steps in the

war that Lincoln feared would be a terrible mistake. When Grant subsequently delivered a spectacular victory, Lincoln was quick to turn around and concede his own misjudgment. "I now wish to make the personal acknowledgment that you were right, and I was wrong."[10]

In the end of the last century, evangelist Billy Graham embodied the kind of humility that guarded against pride. This great gospel preacher enjoyed the praise of presidents and paupers alike. People traveled for hours to hear him preach, yet he resisted lengthy and superfluous introductions. Standing in front of thousands, he regularly made his points by saying, "The Bible says . . . " rather than taking credit for the content of his sermons. According to former *Christianity Today* editor, V. Gilbert Beers, "Billy Graham's secret to humility was refusing to listen to those who would have made him proud."[11]

Pride says, "It's all about you." Humility says, "You have been given a lot of help to get where you are today." One of the ways to lead humbly is to acknowledge and honor that help.

SHARING CREDIT: HUMILITY IN ACTION

David never got to see his dream come to fruition. His vision was handed over to Solomon, who eventually completed the building of the Temple. Imagine the excitement that spread throughout Israel as citizens finally saw this magnificent edifice in all its glory. And imagine how Solomon must have felt as the Ark of the Lord's Covenant was brought to its home in the inner sanctuary of the Temple. It was his shining moment, one that offers us a practical lesson in how to properly enjoy the realization of a dream.

Once the Temple was completed, Solomon did three things. First, he blessed the people: "While the whole assembly of Israel was standing there, the king turned around and blessed them" (2 Chronicles 6:3). He recognized them for whatever they did to help him realize his father's dream. Then he gave credit to God: "Praise be to the Lord, the God of Israel, who with his hands has fulfilled what he promised with his mouth to my father David" (2 Chronicles 6:4). He did this publicly, giving God all the credit. Finally, he celebrated with his people: "On the eighth day they held an assembly, for they had celebrated the dedication of the altar for seven days and the festival for seven days more" (2 Chronicles 7:9). In fact, the Bible says he sent them home "joyful and glad in heart for the good things the Lord had done" (2 Chronicles 7:10).

What a great way for a leader to complete his dream: recognize the contributions of others, acknowledge God's sovereignty and providence, and then celebrate. The Bible does not give us many specific examples of Solomon or David sharing credit, but Solomon did acknowledge the people at the dedication of the Temple — a remarkable and humble act for a king. It suggests that an effective leader cannot ignore the contributions of others.

Genuine thankfulness generates energy that helps get the job done. Turning a dream into reality is hard work. Those working on it need a steady stream of energy. Sharing credit for each success along the way infuses your followers with renewed momentum, and that ongoing impetus creates more progress.

Sincerely recognizing the contributions of others also solidifies team chemistry and leads to efficiency. As trust grows, barriers created by mistrust are reduced, and everyone can move with more alacrity and effectiveness. Celebrating what we accomplish together reminds us that we are not simply a collection of individuals pursuing personal goals, but part of something we can only do as a community.

But perhaps the smartest reason to share credit is that it promotes the kind of vision that results in sustainability. Generously acknowledging the work of others instills a sense of shared ownership in the long-term survival of a dream. Every vision will need ongoing support from both the hearts and hands of those who are touched by it. To keep your dream from flashing big and fading swiftly, share credit with the people involved.

HOW TO SHARE CREDIT

Early and often is always the right time. From the hour you first verbalized your dream, give credit. If you had help from experts to create your plan, acknowledge those essential contributions. Give thanks to the early adopters, the small, risk-taking cadre who believed in the dream when it was still young. And continually recognize the hard work, enthusiasm, and support of the community that keeps coming around the endeavor, day after day, in large and small ways.

Whole books have been written about creative ways to honor people. To get you started, I suggest a basic model: Be intentional. Be specific. Whether one on one, in small groups, or in a public setting, remember where the dream started. Share credit for what everyone has accomplished. Ultimately, name the basis of everything that's been received. Be genuinely grateful.

But perhaps most important of all, create a culture of credit. Name and celebrate good work as part of every gathering, every conversation. Don't just wait for the annual awards dinner. Call it when you see it. Put it on your to-do list. Do it today and tomorrow, next month and next year.

CREDIT THE CREATOR

You honed your dream into a strong visionary statement to guide you and others as you set out to accomplish that dream. You were tempted to start building your Temple, but wisely put in the hard work of crafting a plan. You have accepted the challenge of leadership and with it the task of turning your dream into reality by first seeking initial funding. Only then did you take your dream public, inviting others to join you by providing financial support. Wherever you are in the pursuit of that dream, sustain it by sharing the credit. Avoid the disaster of pride. Infuse it with the energy of encouragement. Create a culture of credit for the work that gets done. Then watch the dream thrive.

And when you finally realize your dream, celebrate the One who holds the world in His hand. Praise God from whom all blessings flow!

SUMMARY

CHAPTER 8 – SHARING CREDIT

THE INSIDIOUS NATURE OF PRIDE

HUMILITY: THE ANTIDOTE TO PRIDE

SHARING CREDIT: HUMILITY IN ACTION
Generates Energy
Solidifies Team Chemistry
Promotes Sustainability

HOW TO SHARE CREDIT
Early and Often
Be Intentional
Be Specific

CREDIT THE CREATOR

BREAKTHROUGH

CHAPTER NINE

STRAIGHT FROM SCRIPTURE

BEFORE I PROVIDE a brief conclusion, I invite you to read the entire biblical account of David's steps for turning a dream into a reality. I have added commentary to highlight the source of certain messages. Hopefully, reading this text again will help you apply it with more vigor to your role as a leader with a dream.

1 Chronicles 28
David, Solomon and the Temple

¹ David summoned all the officials of Israel to assemble at Jerusalem: the officers over the tribes, the commanders of the divisions in the service of the king, the commanders of thousands and commanders of hundreds, and the officials in charge of all the property and livestock belonging to the king and his sons, together with the palace officials, the warriors and all the brave fighting men.

² King David rose to his feet and said: "Listen to me, my fellow Israelites, my people. I had it in my heart to build a house as a place of rest for the ark of the covenant of the LORD, for the footstool of our God and I made plans to build it.

Verse 1 Commentary. David gathered a large group of capable people whom he believed would care about him and his dream.

Verse 2 Commentary. David is now "going public" (chapter seven) with his dream. It might appear that the first thing he did was announce his dream, but as you will see in the rest of this speech, he will unveil the fact that he already completed the key prerequisites of turning a dream into reality — an Inspiring Vision, a Credible Plan, the Right Leader, and Initial Funding.

Also notice how his vision includes all the critical elements discussed in chapter three. It is personal: "I had it in **my** heart." It is succinct: merely sixteen words. It is clear: no one could misunderstand what he was proposing. It was measurable: everyone would know when they reached the destination. Finally, it was meaningful and inspiring to his audience: remember that for generations, the Israelites had been wandering without a home. David is proposing exactly that — a home — both for the Ark and, by symbolic extension, for them. So in just one short sentence, David conveys a dream that is personal, inspiring, clear, succinct, measurable, and meaningful.

Further note that David conveys not only his dream, but also the critical elements of a completed plan (chapter four). He makes it a priority to communicate very early that he has already finished the hard work of planning.

---

3 But God said to me, 'You are not to build a house for my Name, because you are a warrior and have shed blood.

4 "Yet the LORD, the God of Israel, chose me from my whole family to be king over Israel forever. He chose Judah as leader, and from the tribe of Judah he chose my family, and from my father's sons he was pleased to make me king over all Israel.

5 Of all my sons—and the LORD has given me many—he has chosen my son Solomon to sit on the throne of the kingdom of the LORD over Israel.

⁶ He said to me: 'Solomon your son is the one who will build my house and my courts, for I have chosen him to be my son, and I will be his father.

Verse 3 Commentary. David considers his own power far less important than obedience to God. As soon as David communicates his vision and the existence of a plan, he acknowledges with great humility that his boss (God) told him that he was not the right leader (chapter five) for this project.

Verse 5 Commentary. David announces that Solomon will be the leader. He obeyed God and allowed this dream to be executed by someone else. It is very important to note that about one minute into David's presentation, the people knew his vision, that a plan existed, and the name of the leader. David does not risk losing the attention of his audience. He gets right to the most important elements.

---

⁷ I will establish his kingdom forever if he is unswerving in carrying out my commands and laws, as is being done at this time.'

⁸ "So now I charge you in the sight of all Israel and of the assembly of the LORD, and in the hearing of our God: Be careful to follow all the commands of the LORD your God, that you may possess this good land and pass it on as an inheritance to your descendants forever.

9 "And you, my son Solomon, acknowledge the God of your father, and serve him with wholehearted devotion and with a willing mind, for the LORD searches every heart and understands every desire and every thought. If you seek him, he will be found by you; but if you forsake him, he will reject you forever. 10 Consider now, for the LORD has chosen you to build a house as the sanctuary. Be strong, and do the work."

Verses 8-9 Commentary. David endorses Solomon in front of his loyal followers, thus enhancing the possibility of a smooth transition of power. He also challenges Solomon to serve and prioritize God and not himself.

Verse 10 Commentary. Strength is a critical quality for leaders. David tells Solomon to "be strong" here and again in verse 20. Earlier in the Bible, when Joshua replaced Moses as the leader, God said, "Be strong" three times in only four verses (Joshua 1:6-10). Being strong is particularly critical if you have a big dream or a dream for God, as you will certainly face many obstacles. Fortunately, we do not have to rely on our own strength, for as we learn in 1 Corinthians 1:8, "He [God] will keep you strong to the end . . . ."

[11] *Then David gave his son Solomon the plans for the portico of the temple, its buildings, its storerooms, its upper parts, its inner rooms and the place of atonement.* *[12]* *He gave him the plans of all that the Spirit had put in his mind for the courts of the temple of the LORD and all the surrounding rooms, for the treasuries of the temple of God and for the treasuries for the dedicated things.* *[13]* *He gave him instructions for the divisions of the priests and Levites and for all the work of serving in the temple of the LORD, as well as for all the articles to be used in its service.* *[14]* *He designated the weight of gold for all the gold articles to be used in various kinds of service, and the weight of silver for all the silver articles to be used in various kinds of service:* *[15]* *the weight of gold for the gold lampstands and their lamps, with the weight for each lampstand and its lamps; and the weight of silver for each silver lampstand and its lamps, according to the use of each lampstand;* *[16]* *the weight of gold for each table for consecrated bread; the weight of silver for the silver tables;* *[17]* *the weight of pure gold for the forks, sprinkling bowls*

and pitchers; the weight of gold for each gold dish; the weight of silver for each silver dish; [18] *and the weight of the refined gold for the altar of incense. He also gave him the plan for the chariot, that is, the cherubim of gold that spread their wings and overshadow the ark of the covenant of the LORD.*

[19] *"All this," David said, "I have in writing as a result of the LORD's hand on me, and he enabled me to understand all the details of the plan."*

Verses 11-18 Commentary. David didn't just tell Solomon that he wanted a temple constructed; instead, he passed on an incredibly detailed plan, which added credibility to his vision. Notice how the plan includes the designs and dimensions for the Temple, even the weight of gold and silver for the tables and silverware! Every component of the Temple had been planned. Great leaders do their best to ensure that their successors will be successful.

Verse 19 Commentary. David emphasizes that his plan is in writing (chapter four). These are not just thoughts in David's head. They are written down and therefore available for review in the future. By giving Solomon the plans for the Temple, he was generously investing in his successor's legacy.

> [20] *David also said to Solomon his son, "Be strong and courageous, and do the work. Do not be afraid or discouraged, for the Lord God, my God, is with you. He will not fail you or forsake you until all the work for the service of the temple of the LORD is finished."* [21] *The divisions of the priests and Levites are ready for all the work on the temple of God, and every willing person skilled in any craft will help you in all the work. The officials and all the people will obey your every command."*

Verse 20 Commentary. Once again, David tells Solomon to be "strong and courageous."

David also shares important advice: "Do not be afraid or discouraged . . . " David gives his son advice drawn on his own experience. David knows the loneliness of leadership, and acknowledges the inevitability of fear and discouragement, but also the comfort and strength that come from God's presence. As a leader, you should return to these words often because you will often feel isolated and lonely as the weight of decision making rests on your shoulders.

Verse 21 Commentary. David reminds Solomon that he is not alone. He points out that "priests, . . . Levites, . . . and people skilled in different crafts," and, in fact, "all the people" will help him as he embarks on this project. David does this in front of these very people who will be asked to help him.

---

1 Chronicles 29

Gifts for Building the Temple

¹ Then King David said to the whole assembly: "My son Solomon, the one whom God has chosen, is young and inexperienced. The task is great because this palatial structure is not for man but for the LORD God.

² With all my resources I have provided for the temple of my God—gold for the gold work, silver for the silver, bronze for the bronze, iron for the iron and wood for the wood, as well as onyx for the settings, turquoise, stones of various colors, and all kinds of fine stone and marble—all of these in large quantities.

³ Besides, in my devotion to the temple of my God, I now give my personal treasures of gold and silver for the temple of my God, over and above everything I have provided for this holy temple: ⁴ three thousand talents of gold (gold of Ophir) and seven thousand talents of refined silver, for the overlaying of the walls of the buildings, ⁵ for the gold work and the silver work, and for all the work to be done by the craftsmen.

"Now, who is willing to consecrate themselves to the LORD today?"

Verse 1 Commentary. David points out three risks: Solomon is young, he is inexperienced, and this is a great task. He did not try to hide problems. David's honesty and transparency inspires confidence. David does not sugarcoat the challenge of building the temple. It wouldn't be easy. But bold visions and challenging tasks often attract others.

Verses 2-4 Commentary. Before inviting his people to support his dream, David let them know that his own money was helping to pay for the building of the temple (see chapter six, Initial Funding). David's gift was worth many billions of dollars in today's market. Little is more compelling in pursuit of a dream than seeing the leader invest his own funds in the project. David made it clear that his passion was serving "the temple of God" and not himself. David's financial commitment dramatically increased the belief that the project would be completed.

Per NIV footnotes: *turquoise* (verse 2) is an approximate translation of an unknown Hebrew word, *three thousand talents* (verse 4) is about 110 tons or 100 metric tons, and *seven thousand talents* is about 260 tons or 235 metric tons.

Verse 5 Commentary. I like the NLT's translation of this verse: "Who is willing to give offerings to the Lord today?" Only then did David ask for the support of others. If you read out loud the speaking portion of the text, to get you to this point in the story, it takes about three-and-a-half minutes. So in that brief amount of time and only after sharing the Vision, the Plan, the new Leader, and the existence of Initial Funding, did he ask for the support of others.

---

6 Then the leaders of families, the officers of the tribes of Israel, the commanders of thousands and commanders of hundreds, and the officials in charge of the king's work gave willingly.

7 They gave toward the work on the temple of God five thousand talents and ten thousand darics of gold, ten thousand talents of silver, eighteen thousand talents of bronze and a hundred thousand talents of iron. 8 Anyone who had precious stones gave them to the treasury of the temple of the LORD in the custody of Jehiel the Gershonite. 9 The people rejoiced at the willing response of their leaders, for they had given freely and wholeheartedly to the LORD. David the king also rejoiced greatly.

Verses 6-8 Commentary. The people "gave willingly." The word "willing" is used again in verse 9 and suggests that the people were eager to give. David's speech produced a crowd of willing participants and eager supporters. This is exactly the type of support anyone would want when pursuing a dream. It is also noteworthy that the people's gifts exceeded the sum David himself gave. David's formula led to joy among the people as well as for himself, thus dramatically increasing the likelihood that the dream would become a reality. In other words, this ambitious project was not drudgery or a burden, but a joyful experience for all involved. David's "key log" was not money. There is never a shortage of money for what God wants done, especially when yoked with David's orderliness and diligence.

Per the NIV footnotes on verse 7: *five thousand talents* is about 190 tons or 170 metric tons, *ten thousand darics* is about 185 pounds or about 84 kilograms, *ten thousand talents* is about 380 tons or about 340 metric tons, *eighteen thousand talents* is about 675 tons or about 610 metric tons, and *a hundred thousand talents* is about 3800 tons or about 3400 metric tons.

Verse 9 Commentary. The people, having just given billions, rejoiced. Imagine a donor base that quite literally rejoices at the opportunity to give money to your dream!

David's Prayer

[10] David praised the LORD in the presence of the whole assembly, saying,

"Praise be to you, LORD, the God of our father Israel, from everlasting to everlasting.

[11] Yours, LORD, is the greatness and the power and the glory and the majesty and the splendor, for everything in heaven and earth is yours. Yours, LORD, is the kingdom; you are exalted as head over all. [12] Wealth and honor come from you; you are the ruler of all things. In your hands are strength and power to exalt and give strength to all. [13] Now, our God, we give you thanks, and praise your glorious name.[14] "But who am I, and who are my people, that we should be able to give as generously as this? Everything comes from you, and we have given you only what comes from your hand.

[15] We are foreigners and strangers in your sight, as were all our ancestors. Our days on earth are like a shadow, without hope. [16] LORD our God, all this abundance that we have provided for building you a temple for

your Holy Name comes from your hand, and all of it belongs to you. [17] I know, my God, that you test the heart and are pleased with. All these things I have given willingly and with honest intent. And now I have seen with joy how willingly your people who are here have given to you. [18] LORD, the God of our fathers Abraham, Isaac and Israel, keep these desires and thoughts in the hearts of your people forever, and keep their hearts loyal to you.

[19] And give my son Solomon the wholehearted devotion to keep your commands, statutes and decrees and to do everything to build the palatial structure for which I have provided."

Verses 10-14 Commentary. After the joyful fundraising, David immediately and publically shares credit. He praises God (chapter eight). In his prayer, David offers an interesting perspective that is sometimes lost on us: it is a privilege to be a generous giver. He also reminds the people that the money they have just given came from God himself: "We have given you only what comes from your hand." Even though David has just raised billions of dollars, he makes a public gesture of great humility before God and before his people.

Verses 15-17 Commentary. David speaks about an abundance of wealth but also speaks of honesty and integrity: "I gave with honest intent." Honesty and integrity are essential, especially when raising money to achieve dreams.

Verses 19 Commentary. David again prays for Solomon, that the new leader will have the wisdom to be obedient to God's commands.

---

²⁰ Then David said to the whole assembly, "Praise the LORD your God." So they all praised the LORD, the God of their fathers; they bowed down, prostrating themselves before the LORD and the king.

Solomon Acknowledged as King

²¹ The next day they made sacrifices to the LORD and presented burnt offerings to him: a thousand bulls, a thousand rams and a thousand male lambs, together with their drink offerings, and other sacrifices in abundance for all Israel. ²² They ate and drank with great joy in the presence of the LORD that day.

Then they acknowledged Solomon son of David as king a second time, anointing him before the LORD to be ruler and Zadok to be priest. ²³ So Solomon sat on the throne of the LORD as king in place of his father David. He prospered and all Israel obeyed him. ²⁴ All *the officers and warriors, as well as all of King David's sons, pledged their submission to King Solomon. ²⁵ The LORD highly exalted Solomon in the sight of all Israel and bestowed on him royal splendor such as no king over Israel ever had before.*

Verse 25 Commentary. David did an extraordinary job in preparing Solomon for success and modeling dependence on God.

Death of David

²⁶ David son of Jesse was king over all Israel. ²⁷ He ruled over Israel forty years—seven in Hebron and thirty-three in Jerusalem. ²⁸ He died at a good old age, having enjoyed long life, wealth and honor.

Verse 26 Commentary. David's character — built over a lifetime — demonstrated courage, loyalty, honesty, knowledge, and wisdom. This is not in any way a guarantee of "long life, wealth and honor," but it is not a bad recipe for increasing the probability of an effective and impactful life, and of participating in a project of significant historical importance.

CONCLUSION

Sooner or later every person and every organization gets stuck. "Stuck" can be the place where dreams go to die. But it doesn't have to be so.

This book is intended to be a source of encouragement. David's six-step solution will help you break through and push towards turning your dream into reality. These steps require awareness and discipline. They will involve some wise choices and likely the support of others. But they are eminently applicable. If you get stuck, don't give up. Find the key log (the place in the six steps where you run into a logjam). Focus and move forward. If later you find yourself stuck again, don't be surprised. Repeat the process. And if you have any questions on what I have written or need our help in achieving your vision, please go to *counselandcapital.org*.

Dreams are valuable. Dreams are a gift. Don't let them die. Break through!

ENDNOTES

1 Richard Swenson, A Minute of Margin (Colorado Springs, Colo.: NavPress, 2003), entry 175.

2 http://www.dominican.edu/dominicannews/study-backs-up-strategies-for-achieving-goals

3 John C. Maxwell, Put Your Dream to the Test (Nashville, Tenn.: Thomas Nelson, 2009), p. 206.

4 Oxford English Dictionary

5 http://articles.chicagotribune.com/2013-09-25/opinion/ct-perspec-0926-leadership-20130926_1_leadership-great-leader-character

6 http://www.forbes.com/sites/mikemyatt/2012/10/18/15-ways-to-identify-bad-leaders/

7 Geoffrey Colvin, "What It Takes to Be Great," Fortune.com (October 30, 2006)

8 Russell D. Buihite and David W. Levy, eds., The Fireside Chats of Franklin D. Roosevelt (Norman: University of Oklahoma Press, 1991)

9 http://warriorpoetwisdom.com

10 "Learning Humility from Lincoln," by Russell Razzaque, Psychology Today, April 10, 2012.

11 "Integrity Intact," by V. Gilbert Beers, Christianity Today, November 18, 1988.

APPENDIX

THERE ARE NUMEROUS leaders active in Christian endeavors who are worthy of mention. I chose Mark Taylor, Dr. Scott Harrison, and Joni Eareckson Tada because of my personal experiences with them. I believe each of them offers a great example of the embodiment of wisdom and knowledge. They have each amassed great knowledge about the specific field in which they work. In addition, they have each demonstrated substantial wisdom by, among other things, setting priorities, staying focused, selecting people, and most of all, remaining committed to the Bible.

Mark Taylor is the President and CEO of Tyndale House Publishers and Tyndale House Foundation. I got to know Mark by serving on the board of Biblica (formerly International Bible Society) with him. He was also a founding board member and chairman of Counsel & Capital. Mark knows the Bible. His father, the late Ken Taylor, translated the Bible into easy-to-understand language so his children would pay attention during family devotions. That translation became the wildly popular *Living Bible*. Under Mark's leadership, Tyndale House Publishing was responsible for developing the New Living Translation. I have seen Mark function in many circumstances. He knows what he knows and stays focused upon it. He is wise, calm, patient, and able to secure the best from others. He has grown the two organizations he leads in both impact and effectiveness.

Dr. Scott Harrison is the founder of CURE International. He is a knowledgeable and respected surgeon who, earlier in his career, was the CEO of a NASDAQ for-profit orthopedic manufacturing company. He later merged it with a larger similar company and then, while he was lead director, sold it to an equity finance group for $11.5 billion. Later in life, Dr. Harrison founded CURE International, a Christian nonprofit, which created twelve specialty surgical children's charitable hospitals. These gave rise to corrective non-surgical treatment of clubfeet in twenty-seven countries. The pediatric neurosurgical department at their Uganda hospital is the largest provider of care for hydrocephalus in Africa. Their life-changing medical care is paired equally with the good news of God's love for children of all ages. He is wise, and knows how to focus. I was particularly impressed by his decision to capitalize on his for-profit hospital experience in starting and building an international nonprofit Christian hospital network. He is humble, and his progress has been amazing to watch. I was also impressed to see that he was not inflicted with founderitis. He recently stepped down from the role of CEO of CURE in favor of a younger executive.

Joni Eareckson Tada is a treasure. Many know her story. Joni became a quadriplegic at the age of seventeen after a diving accident. Her talents are awe-inspiring. She mouth paints, is an author and singer, and has overcome the obstacles of life with a spirit and focus of serving God and giving help and encouragement as an advocate for disabled persons worldwide. Some time ago, Joni and the board of Joni and Friends agreed that to maximize the ministry's impact she needed to become yoked with an equally talented chief operating officer. She made a wise decision. She conducted a national search and ultimately hired someone she didn't know, a man named Doug Mazza. The results of her knowledge and wisdom are evident as her ministry has exploded since 1999, serving people with disabilities around the world.